SACRED HINDU SYMBOLS

Dedicated
to my
mother
Gauri Chatterjee
&
to my
father
Jyotirmay Chatterjee

SACRED HINDU SYMBOLS

Text:
Gautam Chatterjee

Photographs:
Sanjoy Chatterjee

ABHINAV PUBLICATIONS

abhinav publications

First Published in India 1996
2nd Edition 2001

Publishers
Shakti Malik
Abhinav Publications
E-37 Hauz Khas
New Delhi - 110016

ISBN 81-7017-397-3

Laser & Photo typesetting in Baskerville, 11 Pt by
Tara Chand Sons
Naraina, Delhi-110028

Printed at
D.K. Fine Art Press P Ltd
Ashok Vihar, Delhi

Contents

Contents

Preface

In every religion there are three basic elements: Philosophy, Mythology and Rituals. Thus on the same lines, the world's oldest religion, Hinduism, has all these elements. However, today's Hinduism registers its pulse more on symbolic and ritualistic plane. Thus Hinduism is better understood as a divine way of life rather than a bundle of doctrines and dogmas with ecclesiastical dominance!

The mysticism of Hindu philosophy is unique in its own sense and its mythology is studded with celebrated legendary past which is ancient in nature and current in maxim! This mystic philosophy and many dimensions of *pauranic* legends create a feeling of awe amongst the devouts. But the symbolic rituals gave Hindu philosophy a concrete shape and enabled a common man to grasp its essence. In this context Swami Vivekananda had aptly recorded that "ritual is in fact concretised philosophy...it is easy for men to think but when it comes to practical experience, they find that abstract ideas are often very hard to comprehend. Therefore symbols are of great help."

These symbols are sacred and mystic mantras and signs like *Swastika*; stone images of Shiva, the *Shivalinga*, and of Vishnu, the *Salagram Shila*; sacred rivers and significance of pure water; the auspicious Conch or *Sankha*; the *Tripundra Tilaks* of Shaivites and *Urdhapundra Tilaks* of Vaishnavas; and host of sacred trees like *Rudraksha, Tulsi, Vata, Bel, Kela,* etc., which are great objects of veneration for a devout Hindu. These symbols have an in-depth philosophy and wide socio-scientific base with varied symptoms of ritualism.

India has a rich cultural heritage in diversity and its every region has its own culture, language and social values. Despite these massive sociological diversities, these symbols are worshipped singularly by all devout Hindus and their various castes and creeds. Thus, India is often referred as a country which has unity amidst diversity.

The sacred symbols have come down to us from hoary past and people of every region have nurtured those symbols and rituals in their own way. Thus through the historical process a special meaning and practice has evolved in every region.

In my decade of long research on Hindu ritualistics and symbology I was confronted with its varied nature and differing practices. So I laid a special emphasis to read between the lines of ancient scriptures and incorporated views of philosophers, scholars and historians. However, in diverse literatures there are obvious elements of contradictions. For this reason, I stressed more on actual practice enveloping these symbols and incorporated many a hearsay or *kimbadanti.* Because these are oral mythologies which are being retold from generation to generation by grand old men and women of every family.

My journey, in print, through the passage of Hindu symbology started way back in 1987 when Ms. Aruna Ghosh, Dy. Editor of the famous cultural magazine of this land "*The India Magazine*", inspired me to write a series on this subject. I am thankful to her and *The India Magazine* for publishing a number of articles on this subject which drew tremendous response from people all over. However, in my endeavour to write this series I have associated Sanjoy Chatterjee, who is not a photographer of common run, but has specialised in capturing many rare moods and moments of Hindu symbolism. He, I record, is a national award-winner photographer whose calling is art and aesthetics of Hindu cultural heritage. Without him the project would not have succeeded!

I am thankful to Dr. S. Sengupta who taught me the basic methodology of archival digging and enlightened me about many dimensions of Hindu symbology.

However, I could not have penned my thought without the help, guidance and blessings of my mother Smt. Gauri Chatterjee and my father Shri J. Chatterjee, who not only cleared my doubts but also had expanded my horizon of quest and deliberations. In my process of writing my brother Jayanta served as an instrument of inspiration and helped me to overcome my emotional blockages! Apart from them my 19-month-old son Barun proved a great inspiration to me to strive for this goal. I recall when I was contemplating the whole day to write on 'OM', but I failed to pen down any thought. In the evening my son came to me and uttered 'OM' which was a reminder for evening prayers! But this utterance suddenly made me inspired and I started writing; after that there was no stopping! But I could not have completed this work, which has so varied a horizon, without the help of my wife Dr. Ruma Chatterjee, who not only enlightened me about sacred trees and their medicinal value but also stood by me in my long research hours!

Finally, I may like to record thanks from the inner core of my heart to the innumerable friends, scholars, *sadhus* whose works and words had guided me to this destiny.

20th Feb. 1993 GAUTAM CHATTERJEE
New Delhi

List of Photographs

25. A Vaishnavite with forehead besmeared with Urdhapundra but also sporting Rudraksha Mala.
26. A Vaishnavite worshipping the sacred Yamuna.
27. Sacred Sankha is being blown on the occasion of Durga Puja.
28. Sacred Conch.
29. Five Mukhi Rudraksha tied on the sacred thread.
30. Performing Japa by chanting Shaivite Mantra with Rudraksha beads.
31. A Rudraksha with artificially embossed Trishul.
32. A 21 Mukhi Rudraksha.
33. Tulsi Arati of Vrindaban. Vaishnavite dancing around Tulsi devi.
34. Tulsi Mandapam—a common phenomenon of Indian houses.
35. Tulsi is being offered water for prosperity of the family.
36. Sacred Peepal.
37. Kela Vriksha alongside the Tulsi Mandap.
38. Sacred Vata Vriksha behind the temple.
39. Hindu god Kartikeya.
40. Durga.
41. Saraswati.
42. Ganesha.
43. Sankha.

Signs and Symptoms of Hinduism

Hinduism is a way of life and not merely a religion in itself. Hinduism came into existence not out of preaching but as a result of evolution. With the ushering in of Vedic era in the last phase of 2nd millennium B.C., Hinduism had come into existence. Since then Hinduism has undergone a rapid transition of its theological ethos, social values and spiritual codes. Down the ages Hinduism has thrived with the dissemination of Vedic knowledge. However, one should not take Vedism as mere religious dogma with an aura of magic and charm, but as the embodiment of theo-philosophical pondering, with a scientific base and answers to the man's quest for spiritualism and meaning of mortal life as well! With the passage of time Hinduism has acquired many dimensions and apart from Vedism, many new thinkings have been enjoined to it in its traverse of four thousand years. Thus today, Hinduism has encompassed the whole socio-religio-cultural life of a devout.

Moreover, modern Hinduism is studded with varied signs and symptoms which are mystic in character and symbolic in nature, and are sacred symptoms of spiritualism as well. These symbols are Vedic '*OM*', '*Gayatri*' and Pauranic *Shivalinga, Rudraksha, Salagram Shila, Urdhapundra Tilak* of Vaishnavites, *Tripundra Tilak* of Shaivites, the sacred *Conch,* the *Swastika* and a host of sacred trees like *Tulsi, Vata, Bel,* etc. These are the few symbolic representations of modern Hinduism. However, with the passage of time much of their religious significance and spiritual ethos were lost and most of the devouts follow them as mere religious beliefs and practices, so they never fathom the depths of the symbols or their hidden philosophy, concept and spiritual linkages.

This book is an exercise to unearth some of the forgotten chapters which justify these Hindu symbols. However, before addressing to our theme of the book, we must course through, though briefly, the basic historical phases of Hinduism and ponder over the time and space of these symbols which coursed through thousands of years and their pulsations are still going strong as socio-religious practices of a devout Hindu.

Sacred Hindu Scriptures: An Overview

The Veda is the symbolic origin of Hinduism. The word '*Vid*' or 'to know' is the Sanskrit root-word of Veda which means knowledge. It is said that the Vedas (*Apaurrsheya*) are not created by man and are part of life *Nitya* or eternal. However, Vedic hymns were composed by Rishis and seers under the inspiration of God or the *Param Brahman*. It is observed that Vedic hymns were written by different people at different times. The other name of Veda is *Shruti*, because it is considered so sacred that it is to be learnt by heart only. According to the noted historian, V.D. Mahajan, "The purity of the Vedic texts was maintained as they were considered to be sacred, not worthy to be changed by anybody. Moreover, the hymns were memorised without being understood and when the people did not know their meaning, there were lesser chances of their being changed by the substitution of new words or verses." According to the ancient philosopher Kautilya, "The three Vedas, Sama, Rik (Rig) and Yajur constitute the triple Vedas. These together with *Atharva Veda* and the *Itihasa Veda* are known as the Vedas." Moreover, the period when the Vedas came into existence is known as *Samhita*.

The *Rig Veda* is said to be the oldest of the sacred Hindu scriptures consisting of 1,017 or 1,028 hymns or *Suktas*, which have been further divided in 10 Mandalas or chapters. The *Rig Veda* has come from the word *Rik* or a 'Verse'. According to the famous linguist Prof. Max Müller, the *Rig Veda* must have been completed by 1000 B.C. However, he confessed that "We cannot hope to fix a terminus a quo (*sic*). Whether the Vedic hymns were composed in 1000 or 1500 or 2000 or 3000 years

B.C., no power on earth will ever determine." However, this *Rig Veda* gives us an insight into the social, economic, political and religious life of the people of that period.

The next Veda is *Sama Veda*, which is defined as 'Book of Chants'. This name was derived from the word *Saman* or prayers for singing. *Sama Veda* consists of 1549 or 1810 hymns which are meant to be sung at the time of *Soma* sacrifice by a cult of Brahmins called *Udgatris*. *Sama Veda* shows that Aryans loved music and were 'not merely Puritans'.

The third Veda is *Yajurveda* (*Yaj* means worship) or the 'Book of Sacrificial Prayers', which lays down the code and procedures for the performance of religious rites. There are mainly two parts: one consists of mantras i.e. Black *Yajurveda* and the other is a prose or commentary which is known as White *Yajurveda*.

The last of the Vedas is *Atharvaveda*, which for a long time was not considered to be a Veda as it was similar to *Rig Veda*, but its spirit was different and it addressed to the danger from evil spirits and many formulae of magic to control the demons and evil spirits.

Furthermore, these Vedas are also further subdivided into *Samhitas, Brahmanas, Upanishads* and *Aranyakas*. Sir G.C.M. Birdwood explained that "the *Samhita* comprises the mantras or hymns and proverbs. The *Brahmanas* describe the details of the Vedic ceremonies for the guidance of the Brahmanas. The *Jnana* or *Upanishads* (are) the philosophical part. The *Aranyakas*, belonging to the forests, are intended for Brahmanas in retreat and are closely connected with Upanishads." Apart from these, there are four Upa-Vedas: (a) the *Ayur-Veda* or Science of Medicine and derived from *Rig-Veda*; (b) the Upa-Veda of Science of Music which originated from *Sama-Veda* is known as *Gandharva* Upa-Veda; (c) the Upa-Veda of military science is *Dhanur-Veda* originated from *Yajur-Veda*; (d) *Sthapatya-Veda* or Science of Mechanics and Architecture originated from *Atharva-Veda*.

Moreover, there are six *Ved-angas* or 'members of the

Vedas', composed long after Upa-Vedas. These are *Siksha* or pronunciation; the *Chhandas* or prosody and verse. The Vedanga which deals with the grammar part is known as *Vyakarana*. The *Nirukta Vedanga* is a type of dictionary of obscure words and phrases in the Vedas. The *Jyotisha* is a very important *Vedanga* which is addressed to the ancient Hindu school of astronomy. Finally, *Kalpa Vedanga* is a description of religious ceremonies.

In the chronology of Hindu sacred scriptures, after *Vedangas* the great Epic Era gets attention. The Indologic Epic Era consists of two classics: one is *Ramayana* and the other is *Mahabharata*. The *Ramayana* is the oldest and most popular Epic of the Hindus consisting of seven books and 2,400 couplets and is said to be written by Rishi Valmiki. The *Ramayana* is the story of *Rama*—the incarnation of *Vishnu* in *Treta Yuga*. *Ramayana* is ascribed to the basic Aryan adventure and winning spree over non-Aryans. This Epic for the first time coins different Hindu pantheons which manifested and evolved many Hindu sects and symbols.

The next great Epic is *Mahabharata* which was created by Rishi Vyas and consists of 18 books encompassing around one lakh couplets. The *Mahabharata* thematically deals with socio-political life of the people of that time which introduced many rituals and codes of Hinduism. The famous personality of Lord Krishna who advised and taught Arjuna about the life, morality and reincarnation with semblance of theo-philosophical treatment is of great veneration among the Hindus. These teachings and advices are capsuled in *Bhagavat Gita*. This book *Bhagavat Gita* (Divine Song) is the Bible of the Hindus.

Likewise, Hindu scriptures grew, and every time these sacred books unfolded new dimensions of life. After the lapse of Epic Era (or *Itihasa*), the *Puranas* or legendary histories came up. The other sacred scriptures were the *Yoga*; the *Mimansa* or philosophy; the *Dharma Shastras* or jurisprudence; and finally the era of *Tantra* came into being.

Summing up one can safely conclude that in the Vedas the seers had talked on the one hand about the socio-religious life and times and on the other hand it gave birth to the Hindu pantheism. In the beginning of the Vedic era the *rupa-nama* (shape or form and name) of the God were coupled with natural worship. In later Vedic period we find detailed explanations about sacrifices and life-codes, scores of Gods and Goddesses in their own manifested form came into existence and these were further nurtured in the era of *Puranas* and *Dharma Shastras.* It can be seen that during the period of *Dharma Shastras* several codes, jurisprudence and rituals were coined. Thus from the *Pauranic* time many cults and symbols cropped up which originated from the legendary stories. Moreover, the prominent cult of worship of *Shaivites, Vaishnavites* and the *Shakti* cult came into a proper individual perspective in these eras only. Thus with the individual deities came up several beliefs and practices which are recognised and worshipped today as sacred symbols. Now let us address ourselves to the varied deities which are the source of inspiration of the Hindus and those signs and symptoms which are sacred in nature and ritualistic in practice.

The Hindu Pantheism

Hinduism is studded with thousands of deities, some of them are symbols of main theological cults and some are sub-Gods and even *Avatars* (Incarnations). Such deities are frequently looked upon as manifestation of higher Gods. It is interesting to note that none of the deities is compared because basic ethos of Hinduism is that it incorporates all forms of worship without necessitating selection or elimination.

Since the mythological past these deities existed in a distinguishable form and their distinct physical and personal characteristics find their own singular prominence. These are aesthetically sublime and embodiment of great beauty and grace. Since hoary past these deities have lived as vibrant motifs for the artists and sculptors, and remained an unending source of inspiration for the masses. Let us delve into the formation and individualistic character of some of these deities whose aura still thrives and divinity sparks in the mind of a devout.

Vedic Gods

In the Vedic era we find there was mention of five main deities who are mainly Nature Gods and who touched the cycle of life of man. These Vedic Gods are *Indra, Surya, Agni, Vayu* and *Varuna.*

Indra

Among the Vedic Gods Indra stands foremost. He is the

king of *Amaravati* and of all celestial beings. His domain is the sky and He rides on a white elephant. The weapon of Indra is *Vajra* or thunderbolt. Although Indra carries such a powerful weapon he is considered as a symbol of peace. Indra is worshipped at the beginning of every festival as one of the guardian deities of the world. On the 14th of the lunar month of *Bhadra* (Aug.-Sept.) an annual festival in his honour is celebrated with gaiety in the eastern parts of India.

Surya

The God Surya represents solar energy and is the repository thereof. He is generally referred to as a rude person, seated on a lotus in a golden chariot drawn by seven or seven-headed horses. In two of his hands he holds the water-lily. Surya is still worshipped daily by devout Brahmins. The other name of Surya is Ravi. From Ravi Sunday has come to be known as *Ravi-var* or the day of Surya. Thus on this day Surya is worshipped by every devout. Surya is the only Vedic deity who is enshrined in temples.

Agni

The God Agni is worshipped all over the Indian subcontinent for three days from the full moon of the month of Magha, when the devout feel threatened by Agni in the summer season. The Aryans held Agni, the God of Fire, in high esteem because he was the carrier of their holy offerings to all the other Gods. From the Vedic point of view Agni is an essential part of daily worship. Sculptors designed Agni as a dark man, who wears a smoky headgear and carries a javelin and his chariot emits fire-flame while on the move.

Vayu

The Vayu is the lord of wind and is represented as a messenger of Gods. Vayu looks like a white man, clothed in blue, seated on an antelope, bearing an arrow in one hand and a flag in the other. Furthermore, he is loved as the bearer of fragrance, leaves and seeds and hence a god who helps nature rejuvenate in the epic era. Vayu is seen with his son *Hanuman* or Pavan-Putra (son of the Wind God) in his arms.

Varuna

Varuna personifies the God of Water. He destroys all the demons of the underwater world and overpowers a monster fish named *Makara.* His image is rarely found, but he is worshipped daily as one of the guardian deities of the earth. It is said that Varuna resides in the underwater mountain *Pushpagiri* and rides the chariot on the white surf, with the waves forming its many horses.

Hindu Trinity

In the Hindu pantheon the *Trimurti* or Trinity stands most prominently. The three deities who represent the cosmic phenomenon of life-cycle are *Brahma, Vishnu* and *Maheshwar.* Brahma is said to be the creator of the universe, and Vishnu sustains the universe and finally *Maheshwar* or *Shiva* destroys and absorbs the universe and thus paves the way for re-creation.

Brahma

Brahma is the creator, and is considered to be the supreme God and guardian of the Universe. He is the form of wisdom and knowledge and represents an abstract philosophy about *shrishti* or the creation of Universe. Thus Brahma is the enigmatic symbol of creation of the world. In his image, Brahma is always robed in white and carries the sacred Veda and he also holds a jug of water — the sublime element with which he is constantly associated, because water signifies life, peace and meditative silence. His consort is the Goddess Saraswati, the symbol of learning and knowledge.

Vishnu

The God Vishnu is the embodiment of preserver and represents mercy and goodness. He is depicted as a divine God floating over the cosmic ocean with *shesha-naga* or serpent enveloping the body of Vishnu. Amongst the trio, Vishnu has taken ten rebirths as avatar or reincarnated soul, to preserve the order of the world and sustain the created one. In *Ramayana* he is depicted as *Rama,* in *Mahabharata* he is *Sri Krishna.* Vishnu or Narayana is said to be blue in complexion and sports yellow clothes. In his hands he holds a lotus—the symbol of peace, a sacred conch—a martial beckoning to destroy the evil and the *Chakra* signifying destruction of evil. The *vahana* of Vishnu is Garuda or the mythological bird. The wife of Vishnu is Lakshmi, the goddess of lustre and good fortune. Both Vishnu and Lakshmi are worshipped with great devotion by a devout Hindu. In course of time Vishnu worshippers became members of the Vaishnavite cult. Since c. 15th century Vaishnavites have engrossed the lives of Hindus especially of eastern and southern India. Mahaprabhu Chaitanya of Bengal and Ramanuja of South India were the principal preachers of Vishnu's message. This liberal Vaishnavism had unshackled Hinduism from Brahmanical orthodoxism. Since then Vaishnavites sport Urdhapundra Tilaks and worship *Sankha, Chakra, Gada* and *Tulsi.* Today Vaishnavism has innumerable followers in India and abroad and is considered as the most prominent cult of modern Hinduism.

Shiva

The third deity of Hindu Trinity is God Shiva or Vedic Rudra. He is the embodiment of destruction or Pralay which means that He absorbs the created and facilitates re-creation. He is often personified as *Linga* or representation of procreational process. He lives a life of great austerity and is well known as the renouncer of worldly pleasures and is absorbed in meditation. Shiva is also *Nataraja*, the cosmic dancer and is represented most often as the phallic symbol or *Linga*. Moreover, at times Shiva is referred to as *Ardhanarishwara*—the union of half Shiva and half Parvati or *Shakti*. This symbol explores the intricate relation of existence and consciousness. Shiva is mainly known by twelve different names and resides at different places in India as *jyotirlingas*. By nature, Shiva is represented as a quick-tempered god. Symbologically, he carries a trident or *Trishula* and the *Damroo*—a rattling drum. The *vahana* of Shiva is Nandi or the sacred bull. Down the ages devout Hindus have worshipped Shiva in many forms to attain spiritual emancipation. The followers of Shiva belong to the Shaivite cult, who generally wear *Tripundra* or Trident *Tilak* and *Rudraksha Mala*. They worship *Lingas*. In other words these are the basic Shaivite symbols.

Shakti—The Mother Goddess

Apart from Shaivism and Vaishnavism there is another cult called Shakti which personifies a female energy concept. According to the Shakti school of thought its doctrines and practices are one or more Shaktis or 'Creative Energies'. The *Tantric* school of thought states that Shakti is the deciding factor for the emancipation of man and his spiritual salvation. In Hindu mythology, each God is enjoined with his consort and thus the female energy of every God is portrayed as Shakti. The wife of Shiva is Gauri or Parvati who is manifested in different shapes and is singularly personified as Shakti. She is Chamundi, Sherawali and is also Kali who won over demons.

The Goddess Parvati takes the form of Gauri who symbolises fertility and she is the Harvest God signifying green pasture. Thus she is known as Annapurna—the Goddess of Plentiful Food.

She is sublime and beautiful when she is worshipped as Kanya Kumari in South India. However, she is better known as Durga. This form of Parvati signifies the goddess of power and strength. She is worshipped as the ruler of the universe by whose virtue even Shiva exists. In the form of Durga she holds ten different arms in her *Dasabhuja* (ten hands). These weapons are given to her by different Gods to kill the *Rakshasas* or demons. She rides a lion, and kills the demonic enemies of Gods mercilessly. She is protector of the virtuous and the remover of ignorance. Durga is also Mahayogini and she is the symbol who creates, sustains and reabsorbs the world. In the text of *Markandeya Purana* she is depicted in the *Devimahatya* and called the glorified Goddess. In the eastern India she is depicted as the Goddess Kali and represents the cult of progress. She is black in complexion, who demands bloody sacrifice. She has a hideous face and has the third eye. Her face and body is besmeared with blood and she wears a *mundamala* (necklace of human skulls) which signifies her as a victor over demons. Thus she is worshipped as the ruler of the world on the score of life and death.

Daughters of Shakti

Lakshmi and Saraswati are the two daughters of Shiva-Parvati. These two daughters further the shakti or 'energy' concept but show a positive direction to the life of the devout. Moreover, they, being wife of Vishnu and Brahma, play the similar creative and intellect development roles, in their endeavour.

Lakshmi

The consort of Vishnu, Lakshmi is a symbol of good fortune and wealth. In Vaishnava Tantrism, Lakshmi plays an important role as Goddess Shakti—that is, a central metaphysical principle. Ancient scriptures state that Vishnu and his Shakti are indissolubly associated. So the devouts worship them as Lakshmi-Narayana. Lakshmi is embodiment of beauty and composure and thus she is robed in red saree and seated on a lotus—the symbol of Vishnu. She is accompanied by her *vahana*, the Owl.

Saraswati

Saraswati is the other Shakti goddess and personifies the world of knowledge. She is called the mother of Vedas. Her wisdom is worshipped by every devout. Thus she perfectly suits to be the consort of Brahma—the creator of the created. She is also the goddess of music as she holds a *Veena* in her hand. She is a graceful goddess dressed in white, seated on a white lotus and accompanied by her *vahana*, the Swan.

Sons of Shiva-Parvati

Apart from the Mother Goddess and her two daughters, the two sons of Shiva-Parvati — Ganesha and Kartikeya—are key characters in mythological depictions.

Ganesha

The elephant-headed Ganesha commands wide veneration. He is counted as auspicious on every occasion in a Hindu's life. His wisdom is great and a devout feels that he is the remover of all the obstacles of life. His *vahana* is a mouse and he himself represents the Elephant, thus it portrays that they can live together happily. He is the embodiment of profound spiritual knowledge as the supreme connoisseur of dance and music. Thus Ganesha personifies the intellectual faculties of Gods and men alike.

Kartikeya

The brother of Ganesha is the God Kartikeya. He is the God of War and he singularly champions the cause of war and defends the Hindu Gods. Kartikeya is fully armed and rides a peacock and plays the role of Supreme Commander-in-Chief of the celestial war force. Kartikeya also personifies the Mars, thus sometimes he is painted in red colour. However, the complexion of Kartikeya is yellow and his posture with an arrow and bow is an object of great veneration. In Bengal he is worshipped with his mother Durga.

Sacred Animal Symbols

Since the hoary past warm-blooded creatures of the land, air and water remained a close companion of man. From the days of mythology the animals were closely cherished and regarded as Hindu symbols. From the archaeological evidences it is found that houses and temples of ancient past were studded with these sacred animals.

In the earlier chapters we have seen that all the Gods have some animals and birds as their *vahana* or vehicle. And in the process of time these creatures became a great object of Hindu veneration. These animal deities are: Bull or *Nandi* the *vahana* of Shiva and Parvati. He-Goat is the vehicle of Agni. The Antelope is the *vahana* of Vayu. The Buffalo is the vehicle of the God of Death Yama. Swan is the symbol of Saraswati who is capable of separating milk from water. Garuda the mythological bird is respected by all devouts. Sir G.C.M. Birdwood recorded that "Garuda, the king of the birds, the mystical being foreshadowed by *Arva* and *Tarkshya*, half man and half eagle or vulture is the vehicle of Vishnu, and represented as a great enemy of the Nagas." Apart from these, Naga or Snake worship envelops the life and time of a Hindu. Another mythological animal deity is *Makara*, the sea-monster who is the *vahana* of the Vedic God Varuna. The Parrot is the *vahana* of Kama-deva and Peacock is the bird *vahana* of Kartikeya—the Chief of Army which is divine.

The role of animals and birds finds mention even in the epics and in mythological legends. In the *Ramayana*, when Lord Rama's wife Sita was being kidnapped by Ravana, then on the way the son of mythological king-bird Jatayu had given a stiff resistance and got seriously injured. And Rama could not have won the war against Ravana without the help of monkey-army. In this context of Monkey cult Abbe J.A. Dubois recorded an interesting observation way back in 1897: "The cult of the monkey Hanuman extends over the whole of India. The followers of Vishnu are specially devoted to this deity, but all are ready to give him a share of their homage. Images of Hanuman are to be seen in most temples and in many public places. They are also to be found in forests and desert spots. Indeed, in those provinces, where there are many followers of Vishnu, you can scarcely move a yard without coming across an image of this beloved god." Hanuman worship is very common in northern India and on every Tuesday the deity Hanuman is worshipped with great veneration. In modern days there can be hardly any temple without the image of Hanuman. Likewise, several animal deities are singularly worshipped or revered with the higher gods.

In Shaivism worship of *Nandi* or Bull gets a wide attention. Shaivite scholars state that "the original reason for associating the bull with this god was simple, the great masculine potency which each embodies, and the rage and physical power of which both are capable." However, the Bull or *Nandi* is depicted as a docile vehicle of Shiva and unlike the Lion of Goddess Durga, Nandi is counted as symbol of *dharma*, who stands like a rock. Researchers conclude that "(Nandi stands for) Shiva's ability to burn away sloth, ignorance and evil, ensures the constant renewal of fertility, correct motivation, and religious aspiration; thus he perpetuates the condition in which all levels of *dharma* can flourish."

Another great animal deity is Snake or *Sesha-Naga* who is also known as *Ananta* (Endless), *Vasuki*, etc. Naga is the principal *vahana* of Vishnu, because in the image of Vishnu we find that this Naga has encircled or wrapped the body of Vishnu and the eight heads of Shesha-Naga provide a canopy to Vishnu's sleeping posture. Krishna, the avatar of Vishnu, was also protected by this Naga amidst the turbulent storm over the river Jamuna. Moreover, mythology speaks that

Krishna churned the ocean with the help of *Vasuki.* Since the ancient past Naga represented the cult of serpent worshippers, the ruler of underworld or *patal.* In this cult naga (the masculine) and the nagin (the feminine) are worshipped widely. There are exclusive naga shrines, too, where snakes are kept, fed and worshipped regularly as any other deity.

The symbolic value of snake is considered to be great. In South India, we find women desiring children set up snake-stone or *naga-shila* or *kals.* The cult of *Manasa,* the Goddess of Snakes, probably originated in Bengal and is widely worshipped even today. *Manasa* is a Goddess of Fertility, and may be prevailed upon to cure snakebites. On this score Lord Shiva is also regarded as a healer of venomous infection as he is also known as *Neelkantha* or *Vishapaharana* (Remover of Poison). Likewise several animal deities are worshipped as the symbol of higher Gods. They are not only spiritual personifications but also a great source of inspiration for artists, sculptors, etc. as these sacred animals have remained as a permanent motif of Hindu art and aesthetics.

The Mysticism of Mantra

In Hindu way of life chanting mantra or sacred verse is an essential part of religious rites. No *puja* or religious rites can be performed without recitation of mantra. Essentially, Hinduism recognises the verbal effort and its effect on worship which is more exacting than the physical one. However, ritualistically speaking, physical efforts of worship get enhanced when these are accompanied by verbal expressions and repetitions thereof.

From the Vedic days, these mystical mantras have come down to us, which are said to have been revealed to men by a seer. Thus the element of sound has enveloped Hinduism and remained as verbal symbol. The effective power of correctly articulated sounds is an accepted belief of Hindus. These sounds can destroy, create and sustain the world. The sound itself is the basis for the efficacy of the mantra. It is said that the sound of the mantra has all the creative power, provided the devout has been properly initiated into its mystical meaning and taught about the very methodology of its pronunciation. As a precedence the gate of the religion is opened by the *Guru* to the disciple, and the inner mystical meanings of the mantras are explained to the disciple. Thus, after effective guidance the disciple pronounces the mantras properly and recitation of these several times enables the devout to attain the sublime spiritual aspiration and worldly desires as well.

A mantra may be a monosyllable, as in the case of the mantra called 'OM', or it can be in the shape of verse from Vedic scriptures running into more than 60 syllables. However, in *Tantric* shastras mantras run into 110 syllables.

Generally, mantras are written down in Sanskrit language only, which is the vehicle of religious rites.

However, with the passage of time, in some parts of India the languages like Hindi and Tamil have mixed up with Sanskrit mantras.

Generally speaking, Vedic mantras are essentially meant for Brahmins or the twice-born, while other mantras are of *Pauranic* base and chanted by women and other subordinate castes. For each occasion, Vedic scriptures have prescribed a particular mantra. For example, a specific mantra is recited during *puja* thrice a day.

In the post-Vedic period *Pauranic* and then *Tantric* mantras came into vogue. The *Tantric* sub-cult of Shakti worshippers has fundamentally mystic mantras which find their root in the *Veda* and *Purana* as well. These mantras have a host of monosyllables similar to Vedic *OM*. However, in *Tantra* worship there are mantras like *Kshavm, Klim*, etc. which are secret mantras and each mantra is devoted to a particular tutelary deity. To pronounce these mantras there are specific pulse, pitch, and speed. Thus each individual syllable in the mantras should be pronounced neither slowly nor rapidly. According to the Tantra school of thought the perfect process of pronunciation and pause thereof gain effectiveness as it is more and more silently uttered, and the greatest efficacy attaches to meditation where there is no loud muttering at all, where there is only silent meditation over the fundamental unity.

Apart from chanting mantra during religious rites or *Puja* one is supposed to take the name of the God and count the beads of Rudraksha, Tulsi or Lotus seed mala. And the repetition of these countings is called *Japa.* This process helps a devout to concentrate wholly on the God.

Symbolically, a devout pronounces the name of the deity eight, twelve, thirty-two and one hundred and eight times or more to attain his spiritual goals. A specific name of the God is taken for a particular purpose by a devout. According to the ancient scriptures, Vishnu is remembered at the time of taking medicine. At the time of taking food a devout remembers the name of *Janardana.* When it is bed-time a devout recites the name of *Padmanabha.*

Likewise, mantras are chanted repeatedly and each mantra has a specific significance and purpose. Once the very meaning of mantra is understood and recited in proper sound perspective one attains his aspirations.

Mantra is just not merely a verse but its very sublime audio level creates a sanctified atmosphere for the devout. Thus the element of sound in a mantra is a symbol of a devout's spiritual longing.

The Mystic Mantra 'OM'

In the Hindu symbology the 'OM' is the most pronounced sacred sound-symbol or *nada-brahman.* All the Vedic mantras are product of this monosyllable which, it is believed, existed before the world was created. Thus 'OM' is referred to as the supreme mantra of Hindu scriptures.

Katha Upanishad has explained the very essence of this supreme mantra. It says that "The goal which all the Vedas declare, which all austerities aim at, and which men desire when they lead the life of continuance, I will tell you briefly: it is OM. This syllable OM is indeed Brahman. This syllable is the Highest. Whosoever knows this syllable obtains all he desires. This is the best support; this is the highest support. Whosoever knows this support is adored in the world of Brahma."

In order to understand the meaning, purpose and mysticism of OM, one should delve into it philosophically. According to the Hindu philosophy the world of the Universe had *Nama* (name) and *Rupa* (shape) which are the conditions of manifestations. Swami Vivekananda had perfectly analysed the theme as he wrote, "In the human microcosm, there cannot be a single wave in the mind-stuff (*chittavritti*) unconditioned by name and form. If it be true that nature is built throughout on the same plan, this kind of conditioning by name and form must also be the plan of the building of the whole of the cosmos...The body is the form, and the mind or the *antahkarana* is the name, and sound-symbols are universally associated with *nama* (name) in all beings having the power of speech. In the individual man the thought-waves rising in the limited *Mahat* or *Chitta* (Mind-stuff) must manifest themselves, first as words, and then as the more concrete forms."

Likewise, the creator of the Universe Brahma or Cosmic *mahat* first manifested himself as the name and then as the form of universe. However, behind this there is an inseparable Sphota, the manifestor of World. Swamiji further wrote that "This Sphota has one word as its only possible symbol, and this is the OM. And as by no possible means of analysis can we separate the word from the idea, this OM and the eternal Sphota are inseparable...The sphota is the material of the words, yet it is not any definite state. This is to say, if all peculiarities which distinguished one word from another be removed, then what remains will be the sphota; therefore this sphota is called *Nada-Brahman*, the sound *Brahman*."

Thus the OM which is *Nada-Brahman* or Sphota is the holiest symbol of Hinduism. OM encompasses all the aspects and angles of the creative power and has no substitute. Thus this monosyllable mantra is crowned as supreme in the Vedic scriptures.

Regarding the origin and manifestation of OM the seers of *Atharvaveda* explain that "The super being created Brahman, the creator, on the Lotus. Having begun to think 'by which single syllable may I be able to enjoy the desire, all the worlds, all the Gods, all the Vedas, all the sacrifices, all the sounds, all the beings stationary and moving'. He practised self-control and saw this OM...the all-pervading, omnipresent, the eternally potent Brahma, the Brahma's own symbolic syllable of which the presiding divinity is Brahman itself, with it he enjoyed all the desires of all the worlds, all the Gods, all the Vedas, all the sacrifices, all the sounds, all the remarks, and all the beings...Therefore, the Brahman who, desiring whatever we want, fasts (of) three nights, sits on sacred grass facing east and keeps under control his tongue and repeats this imperishable OM, for him all objects are realised successfully!" (*Atharvaveda, Gapatha (sic), Brahman I, 6-22*)

Let us try to understand the mantra OM's mysticism and its sound aspect. When OM is pronounced we utter three letters AUM. The letter *A* has its own singular entity on the score of phonetics. And if A U M is coupled together, the sound is created from the root within the mouth, and the *U* exactly represents the rolling forward impulses created from *A* and end up in the lips with the letter *M.* If the OM or AUM is pronounced correctly it covers the whole phonetics of speech of mankind. Thus OM is regarded as the eternal bliss and truly symbolises the God.

Manduka Upanishad had correctly interpreted the inner meaning of this OM—the *Nada-Brahman.* It says that "OM is the bow; one's self is arrow; the Brahman, it is said, is the target. One should shoot with all attention and like the arrow he will become one with it."

Likewise, the whole Vedic scripture is studded with one sound, the OM, which has an inseparable name and shape, which is the cause of creation and has a scientific definition of all that man's speech could express.

The Sacred 'Gayatri' Mantra

Next to OM the most sacred mantra found in the *Vedas* is the Gayatri mantra. This mantra is also known as Guru Mantra or *Savitri* Mantra. The mention of Gayatri Mantra is found in all the four *Vedas* where its essence has been explained repeatedly. The *Rig Veda*, the oldest of the Vedic scriptures, has mentioned about this mantra in the third chapter or *Mandala*. In *Sama Veda* this mantra has occurred thrice. In *Yajur Veda* Gayatri Mantra is mentioned thrice. Such is the importance of Gayatri Mantra. This mantra is also referred to as the Mother of Vedas. Moreover this mantra is also termed as secret *guru* mantra by which the Guru initiates his disciple to the world of Hindu theology. Thereafter the disciple sports a sacred thread or *Janau* or *Poitye* and is known as twice-born or Brahmin. The Mantra goes:

> *Om Bhurbubsya! Tatsavetuvarenya Bharga Devasya Dhimahi Dhiyoonah Prochodayat Om!*

The basic significance of this Gayatri verse is worshipping the Sun God—the saviour of all and symbol of eternal peace. Let us become worthy of the creator and to follow him destroying pain of the world and join him in the eternal bliss. God may bless us and our intellect develops and our inspirations sustain. It is said that these 24 letters are the secret string of the inner SELF. If one pronounces it verbally or does the *Japa* mentally an eternal vibration is produced which paves the path of eternal bliss of Brahma. It sharpens the mental and creative ability and enables concentration. This Gayatri mantra has magical power and by its pronunciation the spiritual bell rings on to enjoin life with *Param Brahman* (Supreme Soul). This mantra is prescribed for Brahmins only. This Vedic mantra is mainly meant to enjoin the devout's heart and by means of inspiration perfect intellect and one can transcend to his innermost crust of heart where the Lord resides. Thus this Gayatri Mantra facilitates the devout to reach out to Brahman—the creator, and submerge himself in the eternal Supreme-self, the *Param Atma.*

Gayatri Mantra is also called Sabita Mantra. Acharya Maharashi Dayanand explains that Sabita means the creator. And one who creates and sustains the world is the supreme soul. The *Param Atman* Sabita Deva is the self who can usher in emancipation from the pain of death and birth or *punar-janma.*

Thus, in short, the Gayatri *Stuti* or mantra is destined to make a devout's life free of pains, enchances intellect by its meaning and sounds vibration within. It also inspires the soul to become a part of the supreme being to achieve salvation.

The Sacred Swastika

Amongst the varied signs and symbology of Hinduism the Swastika is the most prominent visual symbol. Generally speaking, Swastika is held to symbolise the progress of the Sun through the heaven. Technically, Swastika means 'of good fortune'—'*Su*' means 'well' and '*Asti*' means 'being'. This is an auspicious mark or emblem revered the world over, since the dawn of our civilisation.

Swastika, the graphic symbol, is found in almost every ancient and primitive cult all over the world. The most ancient Swastikas have been found in the Harappan Civilisation in India, Susa in Persia and Sammara in Mesopotamia. This symbol is frequented upon in ancient Greece, Cyprus, Crete and Rhodes. According to Leonary Von Matt it was a favourite symbol on the coins of ancient Greece and India. Swastika is also found engraved upon the funeral urns which have been dug up in northern Italy.

According to the research of Jamna Das Akhtar, "In Lycaonia on a Hittite monument, it appears as an ornamental on the border of the robe of a person engaged in offering sacrifice. In the designs on jars excavated in Capadocoax, there are found spirals, Swastikas and crosses." According to the *Encyclopaedia of Religion and Ethics* "In company with the thunderbolt and the wheel, it is inscribed on the altars of the Gallic-Roman period. It was regarded as a sacred symbol in Roman England. Swastika is marked on many early Christian tombs." Furthermore, *Encyclopaedia Americana* highlights that "Swastika occurs in monumental remains of the ancient Mexicans and Peruvians and an object exhumed from the prehistoric burial mounds within the limits of the United States."

The implications of Swastika are wide and varied. Essentially there are two symbols: the Greek cross with arms of equal length, and the cross with four arms appearing to rotate in the same direction. However, on the score of implications of the Swastika, scholars worldwide differ and give different viewpoints. According to the *Dictionary of Symbols* of J.E. Cirlot, the Swastika, during the Iron age, according to Ludwig Muller, represented supreme deity. For Mackenzie, Swastika is associated with agriculture and with the points of the compass. Another scholar, Colley March, sees the Swastika as a specific sign, denoting rotation about an axis. There are in fact two types of Swastika: one is the right-handed Swastika and the other is the left-handed Swastika. The shape of the Swastika has been interpreted as a solar wheel with rays and feet sketched in at the extremities.

However, the most general interpretation was that it symbolised movement and the power of the Sun. One school of thought held a view that the Swastika is 'a configuration of a movement split up into four parts related to the poles and the four cardinal directions'. Rene Guenon recorded that it is 'the mystic centre'. It follows, then, that the word signifies the action of the origin of the Universe.

Swastika, a symbol of the cult of Sun-worship, is probably the most ancient cult. The Sun is the dispeller of darkness. It brings joy, light and life for mankind. People belonging to the Indus Valley Civilisation believed in Sun-worship which is evident from the discoveries of a number of seals and symbols associated with the Sun.

Thus since the Aryan days Swastika has remained as a sacred symbol. Hindus use the Swastika on auspicious occasions like Marriage, *Mundan* or *Anna-prāshan*, Lakshmi-pujan, etc. Swastika is worshipped by Hindus as symbol of Ganesha. It is marked along with the symbols of the *Navagrahas.* Thus in the Hindu astronomy the auspicious form of the Swastika represents the celestial change of the Sun to the tropic of Capricorn, and is regarded as a male.

The *Vayu Purana* states that the lord of serpents who lives on the *Devakuta* mountain has hundred hoods which are marked with Swastika or the *Chakra* of Vishnu. According to the *Matsya Purana* and the *Shiva Purana* Swastika is one of the eight types of yogic seats as referred to in *Vayaviyasamhita*.

In the ancient scriptures the right-handed Swastika is associated with the Sun, and hence an emblem of the Vedic Solar Vishnu and the symbol of the world wheel indicating cosmic possession and evolution thereof, around a fixed centre. The left-handed Swastika, which moves anti-clockwise, represents the Sun during the Autumn and Winter, and is regarded as a female and inauspicious. According to the 19th century scholar Sir G.C.M. Birdwood, "the right-handed Swastika symbolises Ganesha and left one personifies goddess Kali or stands for night and destruction." Furthermore, G.C.M. Birdwood wrote in *The Art of India* that "the left-handed Saktas never avow themselves, and the right-handed seldom bear on the forehead the peculiar mark of their sect for fear of being suspected of belonging to the other branch."

Thus Swastika and its mystical significance is being worshipped since the Indus Valley Civilisation, and today on the one hand it symbolises the Vishnu Chakra and on the other it is Ganesha and even personifies the cult of Sakti. Likewise, Swastika has travelled down the ages to become studded in Hindu spiritual and materialistic life as well, and became the object of great veneration.

Symbol of Temple Worship

The whole Indian subcontinent is studded with temples and shrines where a devout Hindu goes to worship. It is perhaps impossible to think that there can be any home without a small place for the deities or there can be any village without a temple. However, it is interesting to note that visiting a temple is not mandatory for the Hindus and a devout visits a shrine or temple on his own sweet-will and not under any socio-religious pressure.

Since time immemorial Hindu temples have come up near the banks of rivers or tanks where the deity is purified with water regularly. And down the generations worshipping of gods and goddesses is going on in an unending manner.

Generally speaking, the institution of temple is as old as the Indus Valley Civilisation. Furthermore, great Hindu temples grew up at places which were made sacred by the legend. Down the ages the artistic flair and technical skill of Hindu architectural creativity got expressed in unique sculptures of temples. On the score of temple architecture an account of 19th century was found where the author described that "Broadly speaking, a temple compound is made of a pyramidal gateway, a terrace, a courtyard with a metallic bell hung on it. The temple building proper has an inner shrine, and within that the most sacred inner room where the chief deity is kept." It can be observed that the room of the main deity is not big, rather is small enough and not well-illuminated. This room is symbolic of a cave where the deity resides. And these deities are worshipped regularly by the devotees.

Ritualistically speaking, temple worship is disciplined and has a strict schedule which is to be followed by the purohit or priest without fail.

Temple worship starts at the *Brahmamuhurtam* or around four in the early morning by lighting up the lamp and ringing the gong-bell accompanied by rhythmic *mantras.* This is the symbolic act of awakening the deity. This is followed by washing the whole temple and sanctifying the same with Ganga water. Then at sunrise the God's bathing ceremony is done privately. There the God is given a bath with water and dressed in fresh clothes. After bathing of God the deity is applied with sandal-paste tilaks. For example, a Shiva-Linga is marked with *Tripundra Tilak* and *Salagram Shila* is marked with *Urdhapundra Tilak.* Then the morning worship takes place with the *japa* and the deity is offered with fruits and sweets.

At the middle of the day *bhogam* is offered by the devotee. This *bhogam* is generally cooked by Brahmin or twice-born only. This *prashad* or offered food of the God is later taken by the devotee as *prashadam.* However, it may be noted that Lord Shiva is not offered with any cooked food, rather is given uncut fruits which become the *prashadam* later on. After the mid-day's meal the deity is put to rest; none disturbs him.

At the sunset *Sandhya Arati* is performed. This time the deity is put on gorgeous clothing or *Raj Vesha.* At the beginning of the evening ceremony the lamps are lighted and drums are beaten and *mantras* are chanted. After the puja, with a brief pause the deity is offered the evening meal and arrangements are made for *Shayana* or the sleeping ceremony. The purohit (priest) prepares the bed where the deity retires for the day.

In day-to-day life of the temples and house as well, hymns are chanted and prayers offered. The priest who performs the puja or religious rites should be well-versed with Vedic codes. However, for the worshipper of Mother Goddess Kali the priest should be trained in *Tantra Shastras.*

In the temples, another important part of worship is the element of sonorous music. In most of the temples the *Bhakti* (devotional) songs are sung which have generally *pauranic* or legendary base and devouts are asked to join the *Bhakti* chorus.

Thus the music is one of the important symbols for Hindu devouts to worship God to the accompaniment of beating of drums and other musical instruments, which are mandatory for temple worship.

The Symbolic Water and Sacred Rivers

In Hindu way of life river stands predominantly sacred in a devout Hindu's life. Prominent among the sacred rivers are Ganga, Yamuna, Saraswati and Narmada. However, before we start addressing the river goddess, let us delve into the significance of water and its hidden symbolical meanings.

In Hindu's life water is essential for the ceremonial bath, for sipping and sprinkling it in all religious ceremonies and is an essential ingredient for offering prayers to the ancestors!

A devout Hindu touches water after every act or stage of *puja* which is counted as symbolic bath and one is to sip the *pavitra* or sacred water at every stage of the *puja* which is a sign of earnestness of intent.

The symbolic significance of water is illustrated by a story which tells how hundred millions of valiant, terrifying giants, though of Lilliputian size, obstructed the Sun's chariot and tried to gobble him up. The gods and sages simultaneously offered full water offering, sanctified with the repetition of mantras, which acted like a thunderbolt on the demons and burned them up. Such is the importance of water. The Brahmins or twice-born are enjoined to follow their example three times every day: early at dawn, before mid-day meal, and at sunset.

Let us now address ourselves to the sources of this sacred water. The most sacred rivers of north India are Ganga and Yamuna which are personified as river goddesses and numerous stories revolve round them. One of the holiest spots of the Ganga, Yamuna and mystic Saraswati, which is supposed to join them by an underground passage, is at Prayag (Allahabad) which is commonly known as Sangam or the 'Confluence'. This place is also called Triveni or the triple braid. Thereafter, the Ganga flows by to join the Bay of Bengal.

The divine Ganga is depicted as a beautiful young woman standing upon an aquatic creature. Some scholars, on reading the ancient scriptures, feel that this appears quite clearly in the shape of the river alligator with long thin fangs. Later on this 'mythical beast, the makara' became the manifestation of the alligator as concluded by experts. Her *mudra* or posture of holding of a lotus and makara beneath it symbolically represents how composed she is and her dominance over the animal. In the hand she holds a water-pot filled with sacred water. Similar pots filled with Ganga water are found in every household and shrine because this water sanctifies several objects and the devouts as well.

On the mysticism of Ganga Hieun Tsang, the famous Chinese traveller, thus recorded between 629-648 A.D. On seeing Ganga at Haridwar he wrote that "(Ganga) is three or four *li* (Chinese measure) wide, the river flows southeast to the era (*sic*), and its mouth is above ten *li* wide. The waters of the river vary in colour and great waves rise in it. There are many marvellous creatures in it but they do not injure anyone. Its water has a pleasant, sweet taste and a fine sound comes down with the current. In the popular literature river is called 'Fu-Shai' (Happiness Water), that is, the water of religious merits. Accumulated sins are effaced by a bath in the water of the river. Those who drown themselves in it are reborn in heaven with happiness, if the bones of one dead be consigned to the river that one does not go to a bad place, by rising waves and fretting the stream (that is by splashing and driving the water back) the lost soul is saved."

Such was the charm of Ganga and she is being worshipped today with greater spontaneity and veneration. Mythological sources spell out that Ganga originated from the sky, and the 'impact of its descent on to the earth to have been broken by the long hair of God', which is often compared to the ranges of the great Himalayas.

Along the banks of the two great rivers, Ganga and Yamuna, one finds many temples flanked by images of goddess Yamuna and Ganga. Radha-Krishna, the much celebrated duet, are always associated with Yamuna especially at the banks of Brindavan and Mathura. This holy land bears the mythological nostalgia of Radha-Krishna on the banks of Yamuna.

The river goddess Saraswati is often identified with the Vedic Goddess *Vach*, the personification of voice and speech. She is also worshipped as patroness of song and wisdom.

Thus the sacred rivers, whatever their names be, dominate the socio-cultural life of the Indian people and their life gets sanctified with their water while the rivers flow by silently carrying with them a mystical mythology.

Namaskar or Pranam: The Sacred Posture of Hindu Salutation

The symbolic obeisance in Hindu way of life is *Pranam* or *Namaskar.* In fact, these are spiritual *mudras* (postures) meant to salute mainly the God and spiritual men. Generally, there are six kinds of *Pranams* according to hearsay and practice.

The first kind of *pranam* is called *Ashtangana*, in which a devout prostrates himself and his eight parts of the body touch the ground. Those parts are: knees, belly, chest, chin, nose, temple, hands and elbows.

However the most common type of Pranam is *Shastanga* in which posture six parts of the body touch the ground and those are knees, toes, hands, temple, nose and chin. This is the pranam which is generally offered to the divine power. According to William Westall, there is another salutation called *Panchanga* in which posture five upper portions of the body are lowered; those parts are forehead, temple, chest, chin and knees. The fourth *mudra* is known as *Dandavata* in which a devout merely bows his forehead to the ground with the hands touching the ground.

The fifth is *Namaskar* or touching of the forehead with folded hands as the thumbs touch the forehead several times as if one is respecting the other by touching the point of third eye or between the eyebrows. The sixth kind of salutation is known as *Abhinandan* in which the person gently bends forward with folded-hand gesture touching the chest. According to a nineteenth century Indologist "When women of equal rank or caste meet in Bengal, they salute each other by raising their enjoined hands to the head; if they are of different class the inferior bows and rubs the dust of her feet upon the forehead." Symbolically signifying that by rubbing dust they could follow the footsteps of the higher classes whose lives are adored by all subordinate classes.

The Sacred Sikha

A devout Hindu keeps a *Sikha* or *Bodi* which is known as *Tiki* in Eastern India. This is a little lock of hair which originates from *Brahmatalu* or the centre of the head wherefrom the fountain of *aura* light glow originates and where *Brahma*—the creator of the world—resides. These *sikhas* are sometimes merely a tuft of hair slightly longer than the rest of the hair. In Southern India, the practice of keeping a sikha by a devout Brahmin is widely in vogue. Generally, one can find Tamilian Brahmins shave off their hair except the *sikha.* According to the Tantric school of thought this *sikha* is regarded as the orifice of the spirit from where spirit enters at the time of initiation and leaves at the occurrence of death. It is commonly believed that before initiation one is as good as dead. This *Bodi* is the repository of spirit because all spiritual energy lies there. According to Vedic text 'Void is he if he is not covered and is clean shaved' because for him *sikha* is the cover for protection. Thus a devout Hindu who sports the tuft or *sikha* can face any eventuality in life in a composed manner.

The Sivalinga: The Symbol, the Mystery

Linga worship has an ancient past which goes beyond the geo-political boundaries of any single nation. Traces of linga worship have been found in Mayan, Egyptian, Mesopotamian and Indus valley civilisations. The linga, which emanates life and light, can be associated with the Egyptian hermaphrodite. In 1925, O.A. Wall drew a reference which says that 'In the Zhob Valley, where small farming groups existed before 3000 BC, a carved stone linga was found...' Also, the Greek god Apollo, it is said, stood for the sun's energy, whose rays had a fertilising and purifying power.

J.M. Allegro records that "The erect phallus was also the emblem of the Roman deity Fascinus." Traces of the linga in its phallic form have been found in northern Europe as well. As Davidson mentioned in his book *God and Myths*: 'According to Adam of Bremen the statue of Freyr in the temple at Uppsala was phallic.' We also find that in Asia Minor the phallus had a cultic significance in many religions.

The ancient civilisations of Indonesia, Indo-China and China also have several references to the linga. In ancient China, the linga was known as *kuei*, an oblong piece of jade stone, which terminated in a triangle. J.E. Cirlot in *Dictionary of Symbolism* noted that 'The seven stars of the Great Bear are often engraved on the *kuei*, probably symbolising space and time.' Another comparable symbol is the Persian Tree of Life whose seeds, it is said, when mixed with water, preserve the fertility of earth.

The cult of linga worship evolved from two basic principles—the cult of the pillar and phallic worship. The cult of the pillar seems to be primarily based on the concept of the Axis of the Universe, which is indestructible and eternally spiritual and which represents cosmic columns in the corridor of space and time. The eternal quest of early thinkers concerned the realisation of the existence of one god. This led to the principle of Divine Support responsible for the sustenance of the Universe.

Reference to phallic worship goes back to early civilisations and seems to be an entirely different concept from the cult of the pillar. Phallic worship highlights the principle of fertility. But according to Dr. B. Patni this differs from the phallic worship prevalent in the Pauranic era. As he says, 'Here (in India) it presents a synthesis of the phallic cult and the cult of pillar—a quintessence of these two principles.'

According to Swami Vivekananda the Siva linga originated from the famous hymn in the *Atharvaveda samhita*, sung in praise of the *yupa-stambha*, the sacrificial post. Explaining the hymn he said 'a description is found of the beginningless and endless *stambha* or *skambha*, and it is shown that the said skambha is put in place of the eternal Brahman...later the yajna fire, its smoke, ashes and flames, the soma plant, and the ox that used to carry on its back the wood for the Vedic sacrifice, gave place to the conceptions of the brightness of Siva's body, his tawny, matted hair, his blue throat...the bull of Siva, and so on—just so, the yupa-stambha gave place in time to the Siva linga, and was defined as the high devahood of Shankara.'

The origin of the linga and its worship has been a subject of great controversy amongst scholars. According to Professor N. Gangadharan 'Some associate the linga cult with that of the phallus. Some hold that linga worship originated from the aborigines of India, while some claim that the association of the Lingatavva with the worship of Siva-Rudra was alien to the Aryans...It has been said that the worship of the tree was later preserved in the form of a stump of the tree (*kandu* in Tamil) which was later replaced by a stone pillar, which took final shape as the linga.'

The word linga is used in many senses throughout Hindu-Sanskrit literature. But the primary meaning of the word is a mark or symbol, even in the context of the phallus, it indicates only a 'mark'. This fundamental interpretation of a 'sign' has always been identified with Siva as his inseparable symbol as is evident from references in the Vayu Purana, Kurma Purana, Linga and Siva Purana.

The Linga Purana, in conformity with its name, traces the origin of linga worship as well as its merits. In Book I, the meaning of the linga in reference to Siva has been elaborated. It says that the word linga is used in the sense of visible symbol. The absolute form of Siva, which is beyond all visible forms, is therefore called alinga (that which has no visible symbol), and is the basis of later manifestations of any visible form (linga). Professor Gangadharan explains that 'The first manifestation for the absolute (alinga) is the *prakriti* or *pradhan* or *avyakta* (unexpressed) as it is called in Sankhya. The matter from which all other categories evolve is therefore the first linga. Above that, Siva is the ultimate principle without quality, eternal, indestructible (*aguna, dhruvya, aksya*) whereas the linga, the visible mark possesses the qualities of smell and such forth and has come into being from the alinga, Siva.'

The Linga Purana also underlines that *prakriti* is a source of the further manifestation of the linga. It explains that of the Trinity, Brahma represents the seed or *bija*, Vishnu the receptacle or *yoni* and Rudra the seedless or *nirbija* (from which the seed has emerged without a cause), but is the cause of the Universe (*bija*). Thus the personal forms of deities belong to the realm of the linga. Above the linga and the alinga and all the manifest forms, Siva is the ultimate.

Sankhya philosophy states that the linga signifies both *prakriti* and *vikriti*. According to the various Puranas and the Saivagams, the linga symbolises the Supreme Being which stands for god himself and is the seat of entire creation and its dissolution.

Dr. B. Patni has analysed the manifested and unmanifested forms of the linga in his celebrated commentary on the Siva Purana: 'The self-existing unmanifested principle manifests himself and again merges back into the eternal unmanifested form at his own will.' He further comments that the linga symbolises the endless process of the cosmic circle of creation and dissolution of the Universe or the micro-cosmic birth and disintegration as seen among innumerable living beings.

In the Siva Purana we find that Siva has a dualistic character, on the one hand he is Sakti (power) and on the other he represents Purusa (Supreme Being), but they are in a singular form of Niskala Brahman (Supreme Being) which manifests itself in the universe and is known as *Sakala* (formed one).

The other question is whether the linga is formless or does it have a form. The *Lingavirbhava* throws some light on this and claims that although the linga has a visible form yet it is called formless. The mysticism justifies the transcendental nature of the linga.

From Pauranic sources, we gather that there were at one time different types of lingas. Prof. S. Dange has recorded this 'lost part' in his celebrated book *Encyclopaedia of Pauranic Beliefs and Practices.* The five main types of lingas are: the *svayambhu-linga,* which shows itself in a natural way; *the bindu-linga,* which is as one contemplates it; the *pratishta linga,* which is installed through proper mantras; the *cara,* which is also termed *abhyatmika;* and the *gurulinga,* which is the idol of Siva.

According to the Linga Purana, lingas are made of different materials. It is believed that they were made by Viswakarma and offered to many gods. However, the six main kinds of lingas are those made of stone or rock or the *sailaja linga,* those made from jewels or the *ratnaja linga,* ones made from metal or *dhatuja,* made of wood or the *daruja linga,* the *mritika linga* made of clay and finally the *ksanika linga* which is made on the spot from any material. Each of these six kinds are further subdivided and when all are calculated the total amounts to forty-four types of lingas.

Interestingly, the Linga Purana lists the various prescriptions for worship for the different castes. While discussing the *cara* or *abhyatmika* and its subtypes, Prof. Dange mentions that the *rasa-linga* is meant for the Brahmins; the *bana* (arrow) *linga* for Ksatriyas; *svarna* (golden) *linga* for the Vaishyas; *sailaja* (stone) *linga* for the Sudras; while the *sphatika* (crystal) *linga* is for all the *varnas.*

Apart from these, special lingas are prescribed for women. Those whose husbands are alive should worship stone lingas, while the *crystal* or *rasa* linga is recommended for widows. However, the *Puranas* maintain that women of all ages should worship the clear, crystal linga.

Worship of different types of lingas yields different results. The *ratnaja* linga yields prosperity and gives glory, the *sailaja* linga the achievement of perfection, *sarvasiddhi.* The *dhatuja* linga helps to accumulate wealth, the *daruja* linga yields enjoyment, while the lingas made from earth help in acquiring all perfection. A further division of baked and non-baked clay is also found. As the Puranas maintain, 'the linga made from clay and baked is said to be superior to the one that is non-baked.'

Prof. Dange referring to the *Puranas* mentions that 'the rock-made (linga) is said to be the best; of middle value is one made from metal; the others come after these.'

Amongst the various kinds of lingas the natural white stone or bana linga is counted as the most auspicious. Bana lingas are small elliptical stones with a natural polish that results from the action of river water. They are most frequently found in the bed of the Narmada River, one of the seven most sacred rivers of India.

Furthermore, the Linga Purana, Chapter I (18.19-22) mentions that various lingas are worshipped in the various months of the Hindu calendar. The *vajralinga* (a linga made from a jewel called vajra) is worshipped in the month of Vaishakha; in Jyestha the linga made of *marakatta* (?); a pearl linga in Asadha; in Sravana the linga made from nila (a blue jewel); in Bhadra one from a red jewel, *padmaraga*; in Ashvina, one made from the jewel *gomeda*; in Kartika a coral or *pravala* linga; in Margasirsa one from *vaiduryan*; in Pausa the *puspa-raga*; in Magha the one made from *suryakanta* (the sun-jewel); in Phalguna the one of crystal. There is no mention, however, of the linga for the month of Chaitra.

Prof. H.H. Wilson wrote in 1862 that in the worship of Siva, the linga is almost the only form in which that deity is revered. In the Keddar Kalpa of the *Nandi Upa-Purana*, Siva says: 'I am omnipresent, but I am especially in twelve forms and places.' These twelve forms, the *jyotirlingas*, are situated in twelve different places. According to Dange, 'these jyotirlingas are various aspects of the "columns of light" that is said to have erupted from the ocean between Brahma and Vishnu as they quarrelled.' Thus it is believed that the jyotirlinga paved the path of jyoti and played the role of universal sustenance.

Somnath (Lord of Moon), the first of the twelve sacred shrines, is situated in Saurashtra, in the city of Somnath Pattan. The idol, which was a linga, was destroyed by Mahmud of Ghazni. A passage from the contemporary source *Rauzat us Safa* alludes that 'The temple in which the idol of Somnath stood was of considerable extent, both in length and breadth, and the roof was supported by fifty-six pillars in a row. The idol was of polished stone, its height was about five cubits, and its thickness in proportion; two cubits were below ground. Mahmud having entered the temple broke the stone Somnath with a heavy mace; some of the fragments he ordered to be conveyed to Ghazni, and they were placed at the threshold of the great Mosque.'

The second is *Mallikarjuna* or *Sri-Saila* (The Mountain of Sri) located in the mountains along the banks of the river Krishna.

Mahakala is situated in Ujjain. According to Wilson when Altutmish captured Ujjain in 1231 AD, this deity of stone was carried to Delhi, where it was broken up. A contemporary source *Tabkat-i-Akbari* records that this shrine was then three hundred years old.

Omkara is the shrine, probably of Mahadeo, at Omkara Mandhatta on the banks of the Narmada river.

Amaresvara (God of Gods) is also in Ujjain. Dr. Hunter in the nineteenth century records this fact. This is an ancient temple of *Mahadeo* situated on a hill near Ujjain.

Vaidyanatha (Lord of Physicians) is located at Deogarh in Bengal. The temple here is a celebrated pilgrimage spot.

Ramesa or *Rameswara* (Lord of Rama) is on the island of Rameswaram where in the Ramayana yuga, Rama built the famous *setubandha*, the line of rocks, between India and Sri Lanka.

Bhimasankara is situated in *Dakini* India. It is in all probability the same as the Bhimesvara linga worshipped at Dracharam in Rajamahendri, Rajamundry district.

Visvesvara (Lord of All) has been for many centuries the chief object of worship at Banaras. Prof. Wilson recorded that 'Banaras, however, is the peculiar seat of this form (linga) of worship; the principal deity Visvesvara is a linga and most of the chief objects of the pilgrimage are similar blocks of stone. Forty-seven lingas, all of pre-eminent sanctity, form part of the pilgrimage.

Tryambaka is one of the principal twelve forms where Siva resides on the banks of the Gomati.

Gautamesa (Lord of Gautama) has also been named in the Nandi Upa-Purana, but the place is not identifiable.

The twelfth and final shrine is at *Kedaresa* or Kedarnath, which is situated in the Himalayas. This has been the foremost centre of pilgrimage throughout the ages. The deity here is represented by a shapeless mass of rock.

Sometimes memorials were made in the shape of lingas. Prof. K.C. Pandey has enlightened us in this direction. He said that the custom of erecting linga memorials dates back to the time of the Bhasa dynasty. Amongst the few memorials whose names figured in the Mathura Pillar were Upamitacarya, Kapilacarya. In this context, Prof. Pandey wrote that 'these lingas had the portrait of the teachers carved in them, seems to find support from the fact that there are two lingas with portraits of Lakuli sculpted in front. One of these is in the temple of Naklesvara and the other is that of Rajarajesvara, both at Karvan in Baroda state. Thus, the custom of combining a linga with a portrait of the person in the memory of whom it was put up, seems to have been prevalent among the followers of Lakulisa.'

Devotees of the various Saivite sects are identified by the symbols of Siva they wear on their bodies. They mark their foreheads with the *tripundra* tilak, carry a *trishula*, smear bhivooti and wear rudraksha beads. Adi Sankara, who advocated the worship of Siva, also covered himself with the characteristic symbols of Siva.

Among the many sects the Vira Saivites are generally known as Lingayats. This sect was founded by Basava in 1167 AD. Historians claim that "They identified the life (prana) with the linga so that they refused to part with it (which) meant parting with life.' Thus Lingayats wear a prototype of the linga on their neck until they die.

The linga thus symbolises transcendental power which is identified as Brahman, and is the centre of Saivite philosophy. Siva is represented in beautifully sculptured forms as well as by the symbolic linga. The linga thus has many dimensions and interpretations. Yet it remains a unique spiritual symbol which does not restrict itself to any one religious order, but is a part of the Hindu way of life.

Tripundra: The Shaivite Tilaks

The practice of wearing Tilaks dates back to the Rigvedic period. Vedic people used to smear several parts of the body with ashes, ghee, etc. after the conclusion of *homa* or *yagna*, which used to be the principal religious ceremony.

With the passage of time, the practice of marking tilaks got further segmented with the growth of Shaivite and Vaishnavite cults, and evolved a varied style of texture which marks their own identical entity. The process of marking several parts of the body with tilaks became a customary gesture and symbolic spiritual aspiration too.

Amongst the followers of the Hindu Trinity Shaivites stand prominent and they mark their body with *bhasma* and *Tripundra* tilaks. *Bhasma* means besmearing the body with ashes and *Tripundra* tilak is a drawing mainly of three horizontal lines with a *bindi* or dot in varied sizes, either superimposed or drawn above or below between the two eyebrows. They are made with ashes and sandal paste of varied colour temperatures, each associated with particular sect.

The 19th century Indologist, H.H. Wilson, noted that "Tripundra" was a triple transverse line made with the Vibhuti, or ashes which should be taken from the fire of an *Agnihotra Brahman*, or they may be the ashes of burnt cowdung from an oblation offered to the God.

Ritualistically speaking, as *Kasikhanda* refers, "Whoever marks the Tripundra with ashes, agreeable to rule, is purified from sins of the first and second degree; who makes it on his forehead without the Mantras, being ignorant of its virtue, will be purified from every simple sin."

At this juncture let us mention the *Bhasma Dharana* or the practice of besmearing. The *Bhasmajabolopanishad* elaborates all its aspects. Noted Indologist and great Sanskrit scholar Dr. T.R. Sharma noted that *Bhasmajabolopanishad* in its prologue states that "I am the Brahman alone, which remains after the illusion of the existence of anything except that the self has been reduced to ashes by the fire, that burns at the time of dawning of right knowledge."

We find in ancient scriptures that Sadhus or ascetics used to besmear their bodies with the ashes of the cremation-ground, which itself is a symbolic act giving a definite direction to its hidden meanings.

In this regard, *Amarakosham* (Dictionary) explains that God is identified with Maha Vibhooti. And whosoever sports Bhivooti or Bhasma inculcates the spiritual semblance of God.

Coming back to the ash one can easily understand that after the death of mortal body, the body would get either the shape of ash or mud. The ingredients of Bhivooti are mud and ash which reminds a devout that his body and worldly desires are temporary and before long it will take the shape of ash and mud after death.

Brahajjabolopanishad pronounces that "Bhasma (ash) alone is the innermost self of all." It further states that "Besmearing one's body with ashes may be indicative of many things. It gives us the impression that the world is perishable, that the divinity is only apparent and not real, that the body is just a modification of earth and that one should adopt an attitude of renunciation towards every worldly object."

The ingredients of *Bhasma-Dharana* and its symbolic spiritual aspiration are explained mainly in two Upanishads, namely, *Brahajjabolopanishad* and *Bhasmajabolopanishad.*

The ash or *Bhasma* is prepared out of burnt cowdung. It is said that in cow's body the Lakshmi goddess resides and so the cowdung is used for the *tilak*-paste. Thus this ash removes the foul odour of human body and purifies the body of a devout. According to the Upanishad there are five types of *Bhivooti* or *Bhasma* derived from particular breeds of cows and having its own significance. These are *Vibhuti, Bhadra, Bhasma, Ksara* and *Raksa.*

Vibhuti was derived out of dung of *Nanda* cow of tawny colour, which comes from the place called *Nivritti.* Whosoever wears this tilak gets immense power and prosperity. Similarly, *Bhadra* types are derived from *Bhasita* cows which are dark in colour and come from *Pratishta.* This type of *Bhasma* destroys all kinds of sins. The third type of ash is derived from the cowdung of *Surabhi* cow which is known as *Bhasma.* These *Surabhi* cows are red in colour and found in *Vidya.* The devout who wears this type of tilak shines brightly in life.

The white colour *Susila* cow provides *Ksara* cowdung which comes into existence from *Shanti.* It removes the troubles of devout's life.

Raksa (*Raksha*) *Bhivooti* comes from Sumara cows of Santyatita and these cows are of variegated colour. Ancient scriptures state that Raksa ash provides protection from evil spirits and demons.

On the score of application of *Bhasma* and smearing of the body we have two main schools of thought. *Brahajjabolopanishad* prescribes that the ashes should be smeared on thighs, private organs and feet apart from the forehead which is fundamental. However, *Bhasmajabolopanishad*, on the other hand, states that *bhasma* should be applied on the neck, right side of the neck, cheeks, eyes, mouth, heart, navel, right shoulder, left shoulder, right elbow, left elbow, right wrist, left wrist, back of the right palm, back of the left palm and shoulder blades. For besmearing of the body and wearing of *Tripundra* tilaks different types of mantras are prescribed which we will discuss later on. However, if one is ignorant about the mantras one can only pronounce "*OM Shivaya Namaha*".

Apart from *Bhasma* a devout Shaivite must sport *Tripundra Tilak.* According to the sacred text of *Vrihadbrahmottara-khananda,* "Beginning between the eyebrows, and carrying it to their extremity, the mark made with the thumb reverted between the middle and third fingers is called Tripundra." There are twelve places in the body where *Tripundra Tilaks* are applied.

Tripundra personifies as *Pranava* (life) and indicates the three activities of God, i.e., Creation, Sustenance and Destruction. In other words it represents Trinity of Hindu Gods—Brahma, Vishnu, Maheshvara (Shiva). Thus *Tripundra* signifies the supreme God himself.

In the text of *Kalagnirudropanishad* another dimensional interpretation of Tripundra is found. Tripundra represents three *gunas* or intentions of man, that is, "*Rajas, Sattva* and *Tamas*". Moreover, these three lines signify *Kriya Sakti* (power of work), *Iccha Sakti* (will power), and *Jnana Sakti* (power of knowledge). The text further states that these three lines represent three moods of Shiva like 'Maheshvara', "Sada Shiva", "Mahadeva", which are the symbolic representation of *Tripundra*.

Tripundra Dharana (or application) and its ritualistic mantras have been eloquently elaborated in the *Brahajjabolopanishad*. It says that Tripundra mark should be worn on the forehead with the mantra *Bhrahmane Namaha*; on chest by pronouncing *Havyavahina Namaha*; on the navel by uttering *Skandaya Namaha*; on the neck with the mantra *Vishnava Namaha*. While applying tilak on the back the mantra is *Hareya Namaha*; on the hump *Shavabe Namaha*; and on the head *Parmamine Namaha*. The mantra *Prityabhya Namaha* goes with the tilak below the elbow, and *Eshanambhyan Namaha* for above the elbow, and for the sides one should recite *Eshandbharya Namaha*. It may be noted that Tripundra should be marked with index, ring and middle fingers only.

In an elaborate research on the subject Dr. T.R. Sharma had explained as to why *Tripundra* marks are to be worn on different parts of the body. Dr. Sharma wrote: "The Upanishad says that by applying the Tripundra Tilaks over the head, one causes all the sins accumulated through various previous births to perish. Sins committed by parts of the body above the throat will perish by wearing the Tripundra mark (over the neck). By wearing the Tripundra mark over the ears will perish the disease of the ears and sins committed by ears. By wearing tilaks over the arms the sins committed by arms will perish, by wearing it over the chest the sins committed will perish, by wearing tilaks over the head, the sins committed by the mind get perished. Over the navel the sins committed by sex organ; over the back the sins committed (get perished). And wearing it over the sides the sins of the kind such as sin of embracing another's wife, will perish. Hence one should make the Tripundra mark with ashes."

Thus *Bhasma* and *Tripundra* save the devouts from various sins committed by different parts of the body. Today there are about 34 types of Shaivite tilaks available and are worn by different sects of Shaivite cult. Fundamentally speaking, there are two main groups among the worshippers of Shiva: one is Lingaites and the other is Shaivites. Lingaites are basically staunch believer of Shiva and they do not believe in Vishnu and Lakshmi and sport a locket of lingam and generally never put on Rudraksha mala. On the other hand, Shaivites are believer of Vishnu and Shiva both. With the passage of time many sects have come up and they sport varied types of Tripundra. Some of them are *Bhahacharman, Vadainal, Vathiae, Asthasahastam, Kanigal,* etc. Apart from these some Brahmins of South India like Aiyanger, Aiyar, Rao, etc. wear a Tripundra Tilak.

Tripundra Tilak has lived down the ages as a symbol of Shiva himself. But today wearing of this *Tripundra Tilak* has only remained as a custom for most of the devouts as much of the meaning is lost to them. Nevertheless, this Tripundra tilak and besmearing the body with Vibhooti is part of the socio-religious ethos of a Shaivite devout.

Salagram Shila

Salagram shilas, it is said, originated from the different parts of Vishnu's body. They are also believed to represent Vishnu's principal avtar. Salagrams are fossilised shells of some extinct species of molluscs now solidified into stone. Found especially in the bed of the Gandaki river, a tributary of the Ganga, according to an evidence recorded in 1590, salagram shilas were also found in the Sone river.

Salagrams are small stones, mainly black in colour with a cloudy temperature, though occasionally one does find some in different hues as well. The stones have one or more holes, with spiral grooves on the sides which resemble the chakra or wheel of Vishnu. According to the *Encyclopaedia of Religion*, these salagram shilas are ammonite fossils.

Geologists claim that ammonite fossils can generally be classified under the Cephalopoda class which is roughly 425 million years old. The dictionary explanation also specifies that ammonites are coiled, flat chambered shells of any of the various now extinct cephalopod molluscs of the subclass Ammonoidea found in Mesozoic formations.

In the beginning ammonite fossils were simple in form, the earliest of which had curved shells. Later they tended to straighten out or remained only slightly curved. According to Dr. P.C. Jain and Dr. M.S. Anantharaman, ammonite fossils have many subclasses and are distributed over a wide geographical area.

While only traces of ammonite fossils dating back to the Upper Cambrian period (around 580 million years ago) have been found, geological evidence shows that in the Mesozoic period or the medieval life of our planet, which goes back to about 240 to 135 million years from the present, these were found in abundance.

For geological convenience, the Mesozoic period, the third era of geological time, is further subdivided into the Triassic, Jurassic and Cretaceous periods. Interestingly, traces of dinosaurs were found in the Triassic period which begins from approximately 240 million years after inception of our planet. Geologist Henry Wood wrote that four types of ammonite fossils were found in this era. These are Ceratites which are discoidal shells, Trachyceras flattened shells, Arcestes and Pinacoceras.

Jurassic, the next period, is roughly 150 million years old. Traces of birds and reptiles were found during this era. Finally we reach the Cretaceous period which is 135 million years old. During this period, geologists claim, dinosaurs reached their peak and then became extinct. Also, birds, as we know them, appeared for the first time. Twenty-five types of salagrams or ammonite fossils were found which date back to the Jurassic and Cretaceous periods, for example the Phylloceras, Lytoceras, Psiloceras, Schlotheimia and so on. These are of different shapes and sizes and are ornamented with smooth or striated surfaces, occasionally with ribs as well.

Just as the lingam is associated with phallic worship, from the religious point of view, the salagram is sometimes referred to as the *yoni* or generative symbol. In the Congress of History of Religions in 1899 (*sic*), Gustav Oppert, a German pandit, read a paper on salagram shilas. He traced the origin of salagram worship to that of the emblem of the female generative principle. He further tried to establish the connection between the worship of the lingam with that of the yoni. Swami Vivekananda, who represented Hinduism at the same conference, refuted Oppert's views and said that though he had heard of such ridiculous explanations about the Siva lingam and other theories about the salagram shila, they were rather strange and seemed groundless to him

According to M.A. Canny's *Encyclopaedia of Religion*, 'Salagram is God and...Tulsi plant is goddess, and in some parts of India the Tulsi is married annually to the salagram. To indicate this union a salagram stone is handed down from father to son as a precious heirloom...Even the water in which they have been washed in is precious.'

Hobson-Jobson noted that the salagram shila was never passed on to a female child, and in the absence of a male heir is handed over to Brahmins. In 1885, Sundrabai from Punjab recorded that 'My father had one salagram. It was a round, rather flat, jet black, small, shining stone. He paid it the greatest reverence possible, and allowed no one to touch it, but worshipped it with his own hands. When he became ill, and as he would not allow a woman to touch it, he made it over to a Brahmin ascetic with money present.'

Females are thus barred from worshipping salagram shilas. Vettam Mani wrote in his *Pauranic Encyclopaedia* that 'On no account should a woman worship the salagram. If by ignorance, a woman,(although being) good natured or of higher status, happens to touch a salagram all her merits earned by good deeds will be lost and she will go to hell.' But when it comes to a male, M.A. Canny records that even the sins of crime can be washed away merely by touching the water in which a salagram has been washed. The *Padma Purana* (Patala Khanda, chapter 20) refers to the salagram as the *padmtra* or celestial nectar of the worlds. It is said that one drop of water of the salagram equates all the merits obtained from bathing in every *tirtha* as well as performing every *yagna.*

Today, spiritualism still prevails despite the emphasis of modern technology. Salagram shilas continue to be worshipped in millions of Hindu homes. Dr. N.R. Roy, a veteran Vaishnavite, says that no worship of god is possible without the worship of salagram shilas. He further elaborates that in the worship of Durga, it is mandatory to first worship the salagram. Thus all Hindu ritual and worship centres around the salagram shila.

Since ancient times man has been governed by two basic urges, spiritualism and materialism. As the *Shastras* stress, the place where a salagram is kept always becomes a place of pilgrimage. According to the *Tulsi Mahimamritya*, the worshipper of the salagram shila automatically gains emancipation from life and becomes the purest of creatures. Its worship thus caters to a man's spiritual urge. However, it is also said that Lakshmi, the goddess of wealth, resides with the salagram, giving the devotee a combination of the spiritual and the materialistic.

Whether in a temple or house, the salagram shila is generally worshipped twice a day. According to Omkarnath, a renowned spiritual leader, a salagram is always worshipped together with the tulsi plant. It is a common belief that the man who separates the tulsi from the salagram will suffer the same fate and will be separated from his wife in every rebirth.

As a pujari once said, *punyas* or fruits are achieved through the performance of *yagnas*, donations or *daana* and meditation or *upavasa*. But the devotee of the salagram shila achieves every *punya* simply by its worship.

The origin of the salagram shila goes back to Pauranic days. As the *Pauranic Encyclopaedia* says, Vishnu had three wives—Saraswati, Lakshmi and Ganga. Saraswati and Lakshmi once had a terrible quarrel and cursed one another. Saraswati's curse transformed Lakshmi into a tulsi plant, forced to live on earth forever. However, Vishnu intervened and said, 'Lakshmi you will live in the world as a holy tulsi and when the curse has been completed you will come back to me. On that day a river named Gandaki will start from your body which will be in the shape of the holy tulsi plant. On the bank of that river, I will remain as a stone image. There will be many worms with strong tusks and teeth, which will pierce the stone into the shape of the Sudarshan Chakra and will create numberless salagrams.'

Worship of the salagram shila has been practised in every devout Hindu house, in their socio-religious functions since the Pauranic era. It is said that those who worship the salagram shila with the symbol of the chakra engraved on it need not have any further rebirths. But its devotee should abstain from arrogance and always maintain a charitable spirit. It is also said that whosoever worships the salagram shila should not attach importance to women or another's wealth.

Pauranic sources indicate that there are nineteen classes of salagram shilas which have also been mentioned by V. Mani in his celebrated *Pauranic Encyclopaedia.* The salagram shila which has one hole and a line shaped like a garland, with four chakras engraved in its cloudy colour is called the *Lakshminarayana.* Another variety, the *Lakshmijanardana,* is similar, except that it does not contain any trace of the garland or vanamala.

The *Raghunatha* has two holes, four chakras as well as a mark which resembles the hoof of a calf. On the other hand the *Vamana* has two small wheels and a cloudy colour. However, neither a garland nor any indication of holes are visible. The *Sridhara* is similar to the Vamana with the addition of the garland. It is said that its owner will be showered by great prosperity.

The *Damodara* is large and round with two chakras embossed on it. The salagram which is round and of medium size is called the *Ranarama.* This has two chakras and marks which resemble a child's kick, a bow and a quiver. The *Rajarajesvara,* which is of the same size as the *Ranarama,* has seven chakras and the mark of an umbrella. It is believed that this salagram grants its owner the wealth of kings.

The *Ananta* salagram is black in colour with fourteen chakras. It enables a person to attain his life's object and helps in the performance of one's duty, earns wealth, fulfils desires and ultimately leads to salvation.

The *Madhusudana* is of ordinary size, cloudy in colour and has the shape of a wheel, with two chakras and the impression of a cow's hoof embossed on it. The *Sudarsana* salagram has only one chakra on it. Similarly, the *Gangadhara* also has one chakra, but the quality of stone is not so bright. The *Hayagriva* has the face of a horse as well as two chakras. The *Narasimha* has two wheels and is of an odd shape. It is believed that its worshipper will achieve self-renunciation. The *Lakshminarasimha* has a wide mouth with two chakras and a *vanamala.* It prescribes comfort to the householder. The *Vasudeva* has two chakras near the region of the hole. It is bright, round in shape and helps its devotee fulfil his desires.

The *Pradyumna* has one small chakra and a hole which has a number of cuts. The *Sankarsana* has two chakras enjoined face to face. Its forepart is thinner than its hind. Finally the *Anirudha* salagram which is yellow in colour, round in shape and bright in appearance, and gives comfort to the householder (Primary sources: *Devi Bhagavata Skandh 9, Agni Purana,* chapter 46).

The spell of the salagram shila spread with the patronage of various Vaishnavite sects. In course of time, however, its worship no longer remained the prerogative of the Brahmin. According to H.H. Wilson, it was Rai Das, a *chamar* and disciple of Ramanand, who revolutionised the worship of salagrams. A dream inspired Rai Das to build a temple dedicated to the salagram shila and proclaim himself its high priest. As his fame grew, the infuriated Brahmins complained to the king: 'A *chamar,* Oh king, ministers to the salagram and poisons the town with his *prasad*; men and women everyone will become an outcast; banish him to preserve the honour of your people.'

The king sent for Rai Das and asked him to abandon the sacred stone. Rai Das agreed but requested that he would do so in the royal presence, since, he said, 'If after being given to them (Brahmins) it should return to him, they would accuse him of stealing it.'

The king consented. The salagram was brought to the palace and placed on a cushion before the king. The Brahmins attempted to remove it but in vain. They sang hymns and chanted, read passages from the Vedas, but the stone refused to budge.

Rai Das addressed the stone with this particular *pada* or verse: 'Lord of Lords, thou art my refuge, the root of Supreme happiness art thou, to whom there is no equal; behold me at thy feet; in various wombs have I abided, and from the fear of death have I not been delivered. I have been plunged in the deceits of sense, of passion and illusion, but teach me to place no reliance on what the world deems virtue. Accept Oh God, the devotions of thy slave Rai Das, and be thou glorified as the Purifier of the sinful.'

As this chanting came to an end, the salagram, along with the cushion, flew into his arms. The king, reassured by his holiness, commanded the Brahmins to cease their opposition. This is perhaps the first time that non-Brahmins were allowed to perform the worship of the salagram without fear or opposition from the higher castes.

With the worship of salagram shilas as its focal point Vaishnavism prospered and thrived. The holy stone is not merely a spiritual symbol: it manifests mystical and magnetic powers, containing, as it does, a people's faith.

Urdhapundra: The Vaishnavite Tilaks

The art of making tilaks on the forehead is a very ancient one and dates back to the time of the Vedic Aryans. Over time this custom became a ritual amongst Hindus and grew in dimension and diversity as each Shiva and Vaishnava sect developed their own special tilaks. This practice continued down the ages and the tilak remained the customary symbol of all Hindus, irrespective of caste, creed and colour.

In the Rigvedic age, a tilak was applied when the *yagya* or *homa* ceremony was initiated. At the end of the homa ceremony, the Vedic people put marks on their forehead, the lower end of the neck, on the arms and on the chest. This mark was made with ashes and ghee mixed together on the sacrificial ladle and applied on the body with the index finger.

Raghunandan, the great law-giver from Bengal, quoted the Mahabharata saying that "after bathing, the tilak was to be affixed with mud and after the homa, with the ashes in order to save one from such sins as the sight of the Chandalas and others."

The famous *Brahma Purana* records that without the mark of the tilak, gifts of cows, offering to the fire, the recital of holy texts were all worthless! The Brahma Purana further records that "a vertical mark was to be made with mud and three horizontal marks with ashes, but a Dwija, Brahmin or twice-born, might mark his tilak with sandal paste."

The Brahma Purana further explains that different fingers of the hand were used to mark the tilaks and the meaning of their application is also elucidated. It records that the thumb was used to ensure sound health. the middle finger for longevity, the ring finger for wealth and finally the index finger was used to achieve emancipation.

From the Vedic texts it is gathered that there were four different kinds of tilaks for the four *varnas*, or castes. The marking of two vertical lines on the forehead which in recent times has become a U shape is called *urdhapundra*, and is only applied by Brahmins. The tilak for Kshatriyas, the *tripundra*, has three arc-like wide upward marks on the forehead above which a circular spot is drawn. The Vaishya tilak is known as the *ardhachandra* or half moon and a bindi or circular mark is drawn at its mid point. Finally, there is the *partal*, the tilak of Sudras, which is a large circular mark on the forehead.

The noted 19th century researcher, L.S.S. O'Malley, in his study has observed that "despite the fact that the Urdhapundra was intended for Brahmins, the Vaishnava generally wore this mark in varied forms while the Shaiva prefers the tripundra which was originally meant for Kshatriyas." His observation proved to be correct and the modern practice of marking a tilak supplements this fact.

In recent times it can be observed that the Vaishnavites are more particular in the wearing of tilaks than the Shaivites. A devout Vaishnavite marks all the twelve parts of the body with tilaks. In addition to the vertical marks, figures of the conch shell, *sankha*, wheel or *chakra*, club, *gada*, and lotus, *padma*, all attributes that Vishnu holds in his four hands, are drawn on the various parts of the body. The many names of Radha and Krishna are also stamped on the body. The four emblems and names of gods and goddesses are carved on wooden stamps with which they are marked on the body.

Different mantras, each especially prescribed for different parts of the body, are chanted as the Vaishnavite applies tilaks on the twelve parts of the body. For the forehead the mantra is *namaha Kashabaya namaha*, for the stomach, *namaha Narayana namaha*, the chest, *namaha Madhabaya namaha*, the neck, *namaha Govindaya namaha*. When tilaks are applied on the right side of the chest they chant *namaha Vishnave namaha*, for the right arm, *namaha Madhusudanaya namaha*, the right shoulder, *namaha Tribikraya namaha*, for the left side of the chest, *namaha Bamanaya namaha*, the left arm, *namaha Shree-Dharaya namaha*, the left shoulder, *namaha Rishekeshayay namaha*, the back or *Prishta-desha*, *namaha Padmanabhayay namaha* and finally, the waist or *Kotidesha*, *namaha Damodarayay namaha*.

It is commonly believed that every part of the body represents a particular form of god and thus every tilak is applied with the devotion a particular god commands.

The most visually prominent tilak is on the forehead. This again differs from sect to sect even among the vast Vaishnavite following. This Vaishnavite forehead tilak is called the *harimandira*. According to the *Haribhaktibilasa*, the Vaishnava authority composed in 1562 AD, "*harimandira* is really the abode of god, for the open space represents Vishnu and the two side lines represent Brahma and Siva." The trinity is thus worshipped. The Purana accepts Brahma as the creator, Vishnu or Narayana is the god who maintains the created ones while Siva destroys and paves the way for creation. This then is the importance of the forehead.

There are vast numbers of Vaishnavite sects scattered all over India. The *harimandira* tilak is as varied in number as in range and differs from family to family and region to region. The tilaks worn on the forehead vary in colour as well and are mainly made from *sindur*, vermilion, *pitta varna*, yellow and *Krishna mrittika*, blackish soil colour. But the main shade is sandal paste which is creamish with a white tone. Turmeric and lemon are used to extract the *pitta* or yellow colour while for *sindur*, lemon is mixed with a higher percentage of vermilion to give it its bright hue. *Krishna mrittika* is obtained from the ash of scented *dhoops*, incense sticks and mixed with lemon.

The Vaishnavite chapter of Bengal was unfolded by the great Indian mystic, Mahaprabhu Sri Chaitanya, in the 15th century AD. Thus the path of *bhakti* was paved for emancipation of the soul. After this many schools of Vaishnavites came up in Bengal.

In Bengal, the Vaishnavites wear different kinds of tilaks which range in number from forty to fifty separate varieties. However, there are six most commonly worn tilaks which comprise mainly of twin perpendicular lines which are parallel and marked on the forehead at the centre of the nose, so that a downward triangle is formed which differs in size. This kind of tilak is worn by the followers of Nityananda Prabhu, Adyaita Prabhu, Acharya Prabhu and Gadadhar Prabhu. They also draw two lines on the forehead but the base is ornamented with motifs of leaves of the *banaspatra* or bamboo, *batapatra* or banyan tree and *tilapushpa* or *til* flowers.

In other parts of India, the Vaishnavite tilaks follow their own traditional fashion. Ramanuja Vaishnavas are more common in the Deccan plateau than in the north. The founder of this sect, Acharya Ramanuja, was born in *Parembar* (*sic*) and studied in Kanchipuram. On the banks of the Kaveri river at Shree Ranga he propounded his philosophy. He then travelled around the country meeting other learned men, indulging in spiritual discourse where he defeated many pundits. The most famous occasion was in Venkatgiri where he initiated a Vaishnava puja in a Siva temple after he had won a particularly long scholastic discussion with the pundits there. He set up many *maths* or temples where the Ramanuja sects flourish till today. The followers of Ramanuja worship Vishnu and Lakshmi in their singular and twin forms. They also worship Rama and Sita.

Tilaks form a prominent part of the religious ritual. They apply *gopichandan* or sandal paste on the twelve parts of their body. They draw two lines with sandal paste from the tip of nose to the end of the forehead, at the juncture of the hair. Between these two lines, they draw another in yellow or vermilion, in the middle of the forehead. This line is called *Shree.*

In Bihar the Ramanuja sect is widespread but their tilaks have a different design. A peculiar tilak, the *bargain*, is worn by the Bhumihar Brahmins of Tirhut. A *Bakra-rekha* or zigzag line is drawn at the middle of the eyebrows from which two straight lines move upwards across the forehead. The base is joined and the tilak looks like a flower held upside down. The *shree* or middle line is drawn in the centre and also joins at the base.

The Ramanandi sect dominates northern India. They are worshippers of Rama, Sita, Lakshman and Hanuman. Hearsay has it that Ramanandi was disillusioned with the Ramanuja sect and his guru, Raghabandra. He left them and settled on the banks of the Ganga at Varanasi. His disciples were from all castes and creeds and some of his principal followers included Kabir, a weaver, Boydas, a leather worker and Sen, a barber. As with other Vaishnavite sects they also worship the *tulsi* and *salagram shila* which are accepted as the embodiment of Narayana.

The Ramanandi sect tilak is a semi-circular arc painted with sandal paste in the middle of the eyebrows. Two vertical lines of sandal paste which are ultimately based on two perpendicular lines end at the middle of the eyebrows where the semi-circular line is drawn. This is called *sinhasan*. The singular line centring the nose is drawn with *sindur* and is known as *agya chakra*.

Another Vaishnava sect is called Achari. The word *Achari* originates from *acharya* which is the name given to the chief gurus. The Acharis are worshippers of the conch, *chakra, gada* and lotus, the emblems Vishnu holds in his hands. Only Brahmins are permitted to join the Achari sect. The Acharis are mainly from the Deccan and are descendants of families who were followers of Ramanuja's philosophy.

Like the Ramanandis, the Acharis draw two upward lines on the forehead. Unlike the Ramanandi tilak, these are not vertical lines but parallel and the *shree* is drawn with the yellow of *pitta varna*.

One of the main sects is the *Ballabhachari* which is predominant in north-western India. They are worshippers of Radha and Krishna, and the child Krishna, Bal Krishna, has recently become very popular. In some respects the Ballabhacharis are considered modern Vaishnavites as Ballabhacharya preached the abolition of stringent practices of self-torture like starving and so on. They have a fairly materialistic outlook and believe in a family life. There are clear instructions that all disciples should offer *mana*, mind, *tana*, body and *dhana*, wealth to their gurus who are called Goswamis.

On the forehead they draw two parallel lines with sandal paste, while between the eyebrows at the top of the nose, the mark is shaped like a half moon. Between the two lines they draw a circular tilak with vermilion. Like other Vaishnavites they draw the conch shell, *chakra*, *gada* and lotus on their shoulders and chest.

Madhvacharya, the founder of the Madhvachari sect, hailed from a place called Ananta Pati Tulab in South India. He was born in 1121 AD and began his intellectual life in Ananteshwar Vidyapith at the age of nine. He studied the Vedas under his Guru Vyas-Deva in Badrikedar. Vyas-Deva finally gave him three *salagram shilas* which he later placed in the three *mathas* founded by him where he erected statues of Vishnu. Udipi is their main centre of pilgrimage. Only a sanyasi or Brahmin could become a disciple by performing *dikshas* or penance.

The Madhvacharis use hot iron blocks to emboss their bodies, especially the shoulders, with the four symbols of Vishnu. They draw tilaks on the forehead with two lines of sandal paste which begin at the tip of the nose and move upward to the roots of the hair. Between these two lines they draw a black line with the ashes of *dhoop* or incense sticks offered to Vishnu. This shyam mark ends at a circular mark of yellow at the middle of the eyebrows.

In Gujarat sects like the *Atibari*, *Bindu-dhari* Vaishnavites sprang up while in northern India, *Harivyashi*, *Ramprasadi*, *Varagal* were the main Vaishnavites. All these sects were formed and named after their gurus. The Harivyashis unlike Ramanandi draw only a singular semi-circular line instead of the round circular spot at the middle of the eyebrows. From this semi-circular line they draw two vertical lines with sandal paste.

On the other hand the Ramprasadis mark two vertical lines in the middle of which they draw a *gopichandan* spot of a bigger size. This is known as the *Beni-tilak* and legend has it that Sita drew this tilak on the forehead of Ramprasadi with her own hand.

The centre of the *Varagal* Vaishnavite sect is in Surur village in the Gorakhpur district. They are believers of the Sanskrit *shastras* and worship Vishnu *shakti.* They are also found in south India. Like other Vaishnavas they draw tilaks of vertical lines on their forehead but they do not make the circular line in the middle of the eyebrows. They draw the *shree* in various colours in the middle of the forehead centring the nose.

The Ayodhya-based *Laskari* Vaishnavas draw a tilak similar to the Ramanandis. The only difference lies in the *shree* which is white rather than red or yellow. The Chattarbhuj Vaishnavas draw similar vertical lines which end on a circular line, but their tilak does not have a *shree* and the space in between remains empty.

The tilak symbolises not only a sect, it is also a way of life. It is an integral element of Hinduism and applied with reverence it becomes an act of worship.

1. Sadhu reading Hindu scriptures.

2. On Om.

3. Nandi the sacred animal.

4. Swastika.

5. Temple Worship.

7. Surya Pranam.

6. Worshipping the River God.

8. Pranam—the devout's sacred gesture.

9. Shikha.

10. Shivalinga of Varanasi.

12. Stone Shivalinga of New Delhi Kali-bari.

11. Snow-linga of Amarnath.

13. Shiva and his linga.

14. Shivalinga being worshipped by woman at home.

16. Shaivite worshipping at the bank of Yamuna.

15. Besmeared with Tripundra Tilak.

17. Shiva-Bhakta at the bank of Varanasi.

18. A Shaivite with the symbols of Rudraksha and Tripundra Tilak.

19. Salagram Shila on a Singhasan.

20. Salagram besieged with sacred flowers.

21. Vaishnavite sporting Urdhapundra Tilak.

22. Widow Vaishnavite.

23. Vaishnavite Saint at the bank of Yamuna smeared with Urdhapundra Tilak.

24. A Vishnu-worshipper performing *Japa*.

25. A Vaishnavite with forehead besmeared with Urdhapundra but also sporting Rudraksha Mala.

26. A Vaishnavite worshipping the sacred Yamuna.

27. Sacred Sankha is being blown on the occasion of Durga Puja.

28. Sacred Conch.

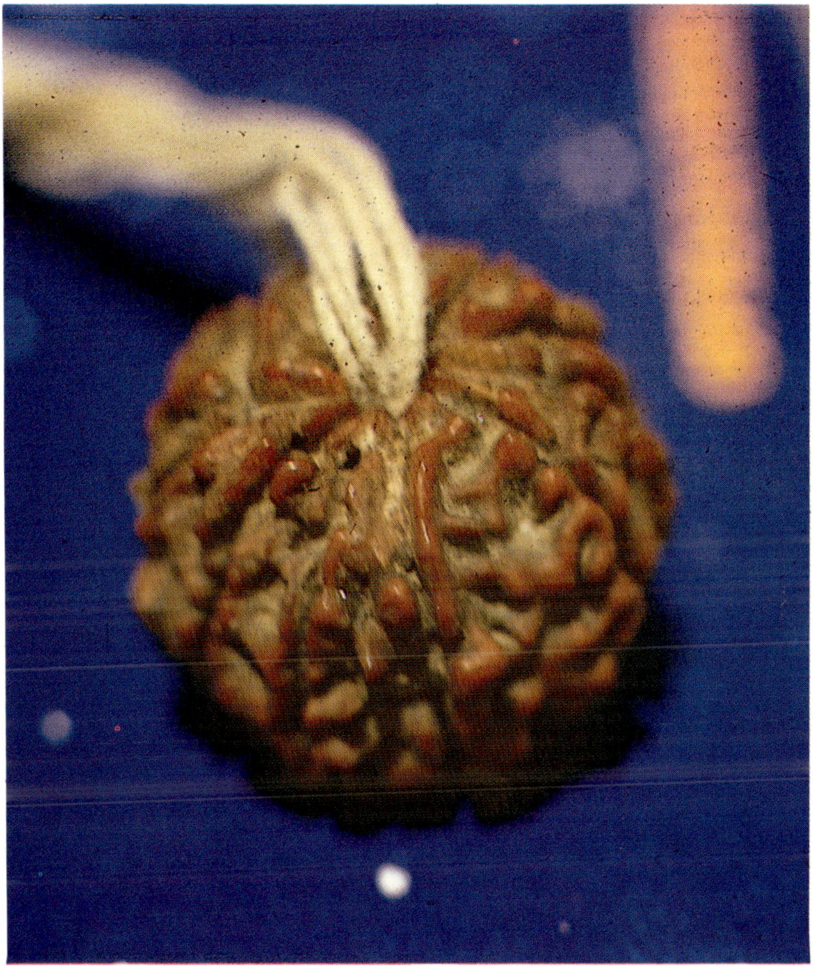

29. Five Mukhi Rudraksha tied on the sacred thread.

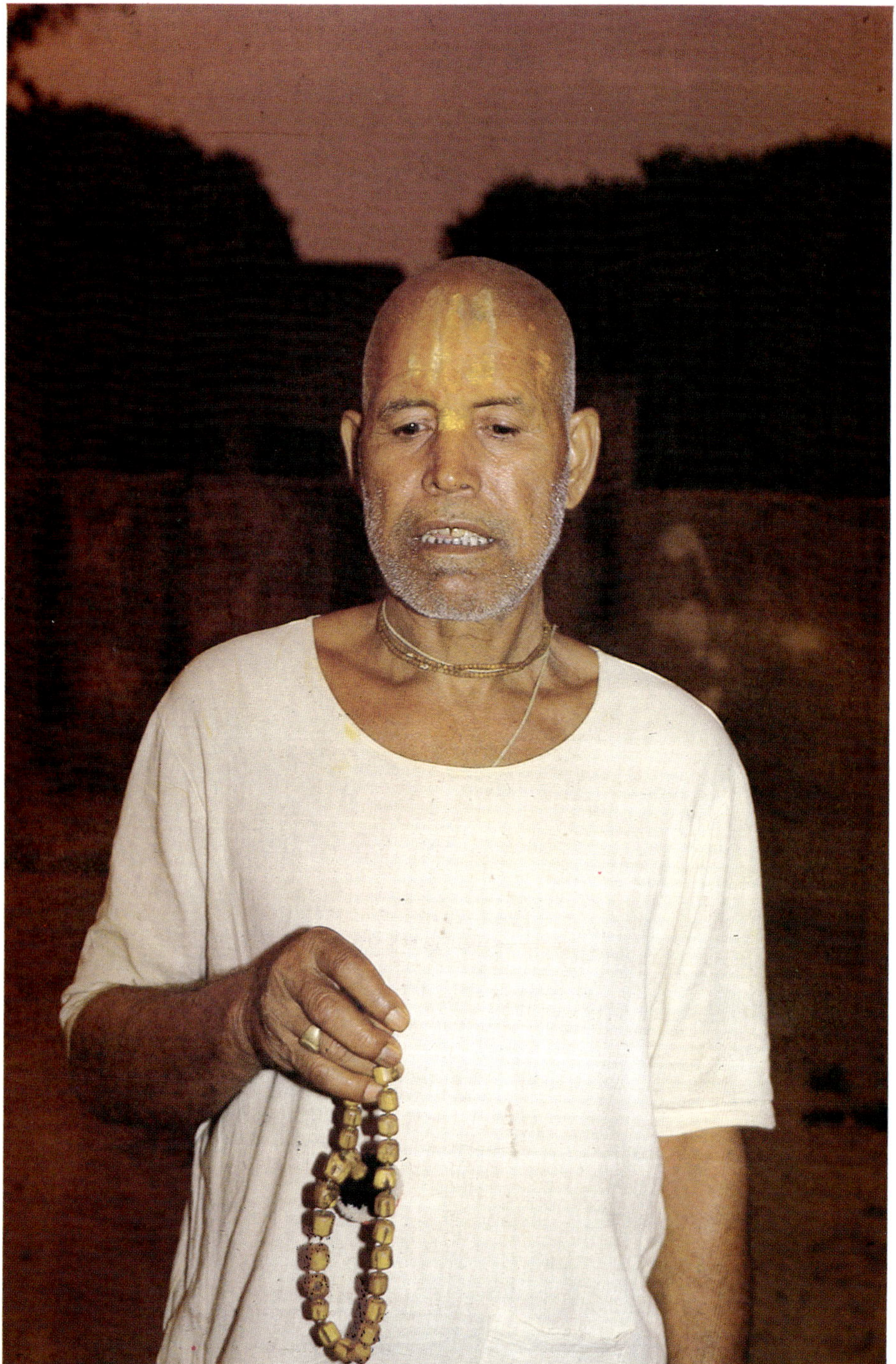

30. Performing Japa by chanting Shaivite Mantra with Rudraksha beads.

31. A Rudraksha with artificially embossed Trishul.

32. A 21 Mukhi Rudraksha.

33. Tulsi Arati of Vrindaban. Vaishnavite dancing around Tulsi devi.

34. Tulsi Mandapam—a common phenomenon of Indian houses.

35. Tulsi is being offered water for prosperity of the family.

36. Sacred Peepal.

37. Kela Vriksha alongside the Tulsi Mandap.

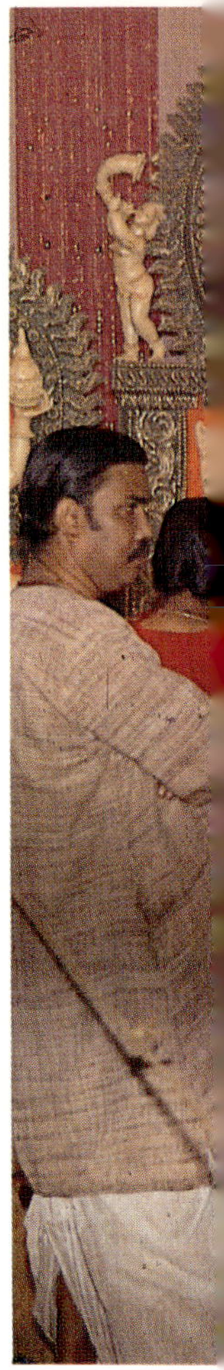

38. Sacred Vata Vriksha behind the temple.

40. Durga.

43. Sankha.

39. Hindu god Kartikeya.

41. Saraswati.

42. Ganesha.

Sankha: The Sacred Conch

Since the mythological past, the Conch or *Sankha* has remained as integral part of Hindu socio-religious ethos. It symbolises the cosmic space of which the attribute is *sabda* or sound. Moreover it symbolises a shape or *rupa,* rhythm and evolves into an elaborate iconography which dates back to its manifestation of divinities in the Vedas.

The resounding musical notes of sacred conch rent the air when it is blown during religious ceremonies and thus the devouts emotions get expressed. The sacred *Sankha* is found in abundance along the side of Bay of Bengal or Eastern Ghat of Indian peninsula like in Puri, Madras, Rameshwaram and finally at the coast of Sri Lanka where Indian ocean finds its shore.

Mythologically speaking there are three main types of Sankha: *Vamavarta* (left side open, it should be counted from the tip) or *Uttar Mukhi,* the second is *Dakshinmukhi* or *Dakshinavarta* (one that opens up on right from the tip); and finally the third type is called *Ganesha Sankha.* The most common amongst them is *Vamavarta. Dakshinmukhi* and *Ganesha* fall in the rare category. However the Ganesha Sankha distinguishes itself with its vermilion outer and inner surface and its short tail.

According to the *Puranas* the *Dakshinmukhi sankha* is the weapon or *ayudha* of Vishnu and thus this *sankha* often symbolises as sustainer of the Universe which is the role of God Vishnu in the divine trinity of the Hindus. The *Dakshinmukhi sankha* also signifies consciousness inseparable from the *mudra.* From arts and aesthetics point of view *Sankha* often symbolises Vishnu himself. Ancient sculptures give this evidence where one finds Vishnu or *Narayana* with a *sankha* held elegantly in one of his hands.

From the ancient scriptures we find there were two types of *Dakshinmukhi Sankhas*—one is male or *purusa* and the other is female *Sankhini* distinguishable with its characteristic variations. The *purusa* got a thicker crust than the finer *Sankhini.*

Structurally the ancient Hindu society was subdivided on caste-lines or *varnas.* Likewise there are references of *Sankhas* classified in four *varnas*—social stratifications. The pure white *Sankhas* with finer surface are termed as *Brahmanas* or twice-born. *Sankhas* having rougher surface with reddish or brownish colour temperatures are called *Kshatriyas* (the warrior class). The Sankhas with glossy surface and light yellow in colour are known as *Vaishyas* (the business community). Finally the hard dull grey-coloured Sankhas are categorised as *Sudra Sankhas.*

Ancient scriptures like the *Mahabharata, Ramayana* and *Puranas/Upa-puranas* have eulogised sankha which encapsules the aura of spiritual aspiration and veneration which lived down the ages as symbol aesthetics and theosophy. The sankha is basically an integral part of Vaishnavite symbology. The practice of wearing tilaks in the shape of Sankha is in vogue since the days of *Ramanujam.*

In the legendary past we find that during the *Samundra Manthana* or churning of the ocean the *sankha* was used and remained an object of benefaction. The God of Wealth in Hindu mythology is *Kuber* who is said to be in possession of eight auspicious jewels and one of them was *Sankhanidhi.* On the score of snake worship this Sankha is counted as one of the *astangas*—serpent gods of eminence.

Apart from *Sankha* being a spiritual symbol it also played a vital role in the warfare of ancient glory and was counted as a marshal factor. In the epic era the sankha remained an integral part of warfare. And wars used to be restricted to day time only. Thus the blowing of Sankha at sunrise meant that war was on and again Sankha used to be blown at dusk signifying retreat to the camps for night rest. Sankha used to signify victory signal as well. Moreover in the marshal formation Sankha played a very vital role.

In the *Mahabharata* we find that *Sankha* or conch shell had different names. The *Sankha* of Lord Krishna was called *Panchajanya.* The divine *Sankha* of Arjuna was *Devadutta.* Yudhistra's and Bheema's sacred *sankhas* were known as *Anantavijaya* and *Paundra* respectively. The *Manipuspaka* conch was of Sahadeva, while the divine sankha of Nakula was *Sughosh.*

The *Sankha's* varied musical intonation of different pitches and frequency of sound signified particular meaning. On the score of blowing of *sankha* there are mainly two processes. One is by holding the mouth of the conch or the drilled tip directly to the lips which is known as *dhamana.* The second one is by connecting the drilled tip to an ornamental brass pipe which is commonly known as *purana.* In the process of blowing *sankha* one controls his breath and a slower and rhythmic flow of air current produced a harmonic effect which is called *Sankhadhwani.*

Ritualistically speaking *sankha* is an essential part of Hindu way of life. It is customary in a Hindu household specially in a Brahmin's house to blow *sankha* three times a day or *Tin Sandhya* accompanied by *Gayatri Japa.* In temple worship also the Sankha is blown during the *Nitya puja* (daily worship) accompanied by other musical instruments like *Kansar* (a plate of bronze beaten rhythmically with *chandan* or sandalwood).

According to hearsay the sound of *sankha* produces a frequency which creates an uneasiness or an erratic sensation in animals. So if sankha is blown none of the deadly animals like snakes can come close to the place of worship and devouts can concentrate on God safely. It is also believed that the sound of sankha keeps away the evil spirits. On this score the practice of blowing *sankha* during earthquake or natural calamities is still in vogue especially in eastern India. This signifies that a devout is calling upon Vishnu, the sustainer of the Universe and keeping the snakes etc. away from houses.

The *sankha* has manifold *ayurvedic* or medicinal significance too. According to the *Vaidya Shastras* it has great medicinal value. Its judicious preparation alleviates many ailments.

The *Sankha* was never encapsuled in spiritual veneration only rather it lived as an auspicious sound which envelops the ceremonies like New Year or *Nava-Varsha*, birth, *Annaprasana*, *Upanayana*, marriage and death too. Since hoary past the practice of blowing sankha on the occasion of bidding farewell to seafaring kinsmen is prevailing amongst the *Sadhaba* community of Orissa. During October-November the population of Tanjavur district of Tamil Nadu celebrates *Samkabhisekam*. On this occasion one thousand and eight conches are taken out in procession. The conch shells are filled with water and assembled at Amritaghateswar temple for *abhishekam* or coronation. The water in the shell is considered as sacred where god dwells.

Sankha filled with water is an essential part of *arati* during Durga Puja in Bengal. It may not be out of place to mention that Sankha in Puri of Orissa is known as *Samkha Khetra* because there conch shells are found in abundance. During the famous *Ratha Yatra*, Subhadra, the sister of Jagannath and Baldeva, is seated on *Samkhanavi Mandal*.

Likewise Sankha has lived down the ages as an embodiment of spiritual aspirations and as socio-cultural ethos of Hinduism. This has remained as musical sensation with its marshal and spiritual intonations. Furthermore the Sankha is part of Hindu aesthetics as we find that from ancient days sculptors and artists made this sankha a permanent motif in stone carvings and canvases as well.

The Symbolism of Sacred Trees

Hinduism is studded with varied signs and symptoms which are mystic in character and symbolic in nature. These are embodiment of ever continuing ecclesiastical spirit and part of the socio-cultural ethos. Amongst the various sacred symbols plants and trees stand prominent. Since the hoary past tree worship is in vogue across the culture, race and civilisation scaling beyond geo-political boundary. Centring around venerated trees the mankind explored its inner faculties like Art, Philosophy and Religion which manifested itself in symbolic representation, throughout the world, in its motifs and living forms of sacred trees.

Ritualistic veneration of trees is common worldwide as we find animated trees in the text of Pyramids and the most popular holy tree known to ancient Egyptians was *Tamarisk.* In Japan, around 900 years ago, a Buddhist nun planted a tree named *Shimonishimura.* It is said that whosoever eats with chop-sticks made from the wood of this miraculous tree would never have toothache.

Dr. S. Sen, the celebrated researcher on 'sacred' trees, noted that "The Africans believe that gods inhabit in certain kinds of trees which are never cut with an axe. In Bavaria, there is a tree that brings good luck to newly-wed couples, if they will go and sit under its branches after midnight."

Some evidences are found that when tree-spirit is displeased with its worshippers then calamity befalls upon them. According to *Encyclopaedia of Superstition and Folklore* similar thing happened in Sri Lanka when a worst storm lashed and raged the country and uprooted the sacred Bo-tree which is identified with Lord Krishna. In the Bhagavat Gita this Bo-tree is regarded as the abode of Hindu Trinity—Brahma, Vishnu and Maheshwar. The earliest historical reference to Sri Lanka's Bo-tree was found in the travelogue of Fahian, a Chinese visitor, who visited the tree in 414 AD and wrote that this tree was planted way back in 288 BC by King Devinpattsa. It is widely believed that this tree was the branch of *Bodhi* tree of Bodhgaya whereunder Lord Buddha had attained *Nirvana.*

In many places it is considered that cutting down a sacred tree is dangerous and inauspicious as tree-god or tree-spirit might become angry and revengeful. For this reason since ancient days in India trees were worshipped before cutting down. According to the *Brihatsamhita* before taking wood from a particular tree which must be used for making images of Gods, the people of four *varnas* should invoke those trees after the worship at night with a prayer in these words:

> "O tree! We are interested in making an image of a deity. I salute you. Please accept my worship offered according to injunctions, may those beings who reside here arrange for their residence elsewhere after accepting the injunctions. Let them forgive me!"

Likewise trees were worshipped as a symbol of God and Spirit which were only to be realised by heart. Thus was the humble beginning of nature-worship encircling trees.

In this regard, the famous Hindu law-giver Manu stated that "All trees and plants are full of consciousness within themselves and are endowed with the feeling of pleasures and pain." Furthermore, the *Upanishad* declares that "The God who exists in this Universe, in water, in fire also exists in large trees and herbs."

Swami Vivekananda had rightly explained while speaking on '*Karma Yoga*' that in every religion there are three essential parts—philosophy, mythology and rituals. Philosophy is the essence of religion and mythology illustrates them with the help of legends, stories. Finally, Swamiji said that the rituals give that philosophy a concrete shape and enable common man to grasp. Vivekananda recorded that "ritual is in fact concretised philosophy...It is easy for men to think that they understand anything; but when it comes to practical experience, they find that abstract ideas are often very hard to comprehend. Therefore symbols are of great help." Thus from time immemorial symbols have been used by all religions across the world.

The role of sacred trees, plants and their leaves stands foremost in the ritualistic life of Hindus and they have medicinal value as well. There are numerous valuable plants and trees available in the tropical Indian subcontinent. But we take up a few prominent tree symbols which are being theosophically nurtured and no puja or worship is possible without them.

Rudraksha: The Tears of Shiva

The most powerful deity in the Trinity is Rudra whose aura spreads an enigmatic spell over the Hindu mythology. The first reference to Rudra is found in the *Rigveda.* This culminated into a full-fledged character, Shiva, in the later days of the *Puranas.* The word Rudra originated from the Sanskrit *rud* or *rodden* which means to cry or crying, thus Rudra is one who cries. According to the *Devi Bhagavata Skandha 7,* Rudra was born from the fury of Brahma. The story of Rudra's birth can be traced from the *Pauranic Encyclopaedia* where it is said that even before the creation of *Prajapatis,* Brahma created Sanandana, Sanaka, Sanatana and Sanatkumara. Unfortunately these four beings were not interested in progeny. This made Brahma furious and he was prepared to destroy the three worlds, *Swarga, Marta* and *Patal.* The three worlds shone in the radiance that emanated from the fire of Brahma's fury. From his shining eyebrows, curved with anger, a figure of unbearable radiance appeared. This was the birth of Rudra who had three eyes, a blue complexion and cried continuously. Brahma asked him, "Why are you crying?" and the boy replied: "I must be named", and he was given seven other names, Bhava, Sarava, Isana, Pashupati, Bhima, Ugar and Mahadeva. Rudra is thus called by eight names.

Rudraksha means the tears and eyes of Rudra. In the last century John Garrett traced that 'the meaning of the world is Rudra's (Shiva's) eye (*Akshu*) and then also tears (*Rud*).' One school of thought believes that Shiva, during a war with the *asuras* or demons, having burned three cities, wept at the loss of lives. The tears that fell on the ground sprang up as shrubs, producing berries which were called rudraksha.

The rudraksha has always been an important symbol in the Hindu way of life. Interpreting Shastras Swami Prabhanandgiri said that "whosoever wears the rudraksha mala, after death he never goes to *yonilok* or circle of rebirth, rather he gets *shivalok.*" According to *Rudrakshajabolopanishad*, "The man (wearer of the Rudraksha) should abstain from spirituous liquor, flesh, garlic, onions, raddish, the fruit of the Slesmakata tree (tamarisk) and Vidavatha." And who follows all these gets emancipation through the Rudraksha.

An incident in the *Devi Bhagavata Skandha 11* explains how the rudraksha came to be honoured in the Hindu way of life. Once there lived an *asura* chief who was mighty and valiant. His name was Tripura. He defeated the Devas (gods) and Deva Chief and became emperor of the asuras. The Devas (gods) were very grieved and went to Shiva. Then Shiva thought for a while, on how to kill Tripura. With open eyes, he sat for a thousand divine years or thirty-six lakh human years. After this prolonged length of time, Shiva winked his eyes and tears fell from them. The rudraksha tree grew from these tears. Twelve types of rudraksha came into being from the Sun, and from Moon emerged sixteen kinds of rudraksha and finally from the Fire came ten kinds of rudraksha. Those which originated from the Sun are of blood colour, those from the Moon are white and those from the Fire are black. Moreover, the *Rudrakshajabolopanishad* states that Rudrakshas are also classified according to the four castes or *Varnas*, viz., Brahmana, Ksatriya, Vaisya and Sudra. An authority, Dr. T.R. Sharma, noted that "Those four trees bore four beads of white, red, tawny and black colours. Thus, the Brahmanas should use white beads, the Ksatriyas should use the red beads, the Vaisyas should use the tawny-coloured beads and the Sudras should use the black ones."

The rudraksha tree is one of the many species of flora which belong to the *Elaeocarpus* family, which according to the *Wealth of India, 1952,* is 'a large genus of trees distributed from south and east Asia through Malaysia to Australia and the

Pacific Island.' In the Indian subcontinent these trees are found primarily in Nepal. Other sources record that the trees from the Elaeocarpus family are found in Nepal, Bihar, Bengal, Assam, Madhya Pradesh and Bombay. Amongst the various types some twenty-five species are found in India. These are mainly *Elaeocarpus ferrugineus, Elaeocarpus lanceacfolius roxb, Elaeocarpus serratus linn, Elaeocarpus tuberculatus roxb* and others. However, the rudraksha is specifically identified as the *Elaeocarpus ganitrus roxb.* In 1906 Dietrich Brandis wrote that the rudraksha tree grows to a height of sixty feet. It has white flowers which are shorter than its leaves. According to the CSIR Dictionary of Flora the tree has oblong leaves and the flowers emerge from the old leaf axils, the fruits are 'drupes deep or bluish purple, globose or obovoid enclosing a hard, longitudinally grooved, tuberclad, normally five-celled, mukhee, stone.' Consequently Dietrich Brandis recorded in the *Indian Tree* that the fruits are spherical and hard and have varied sizes which range from three quarter to an inch in diameter. The *Tantra Shastra* claims that the smaller rudraksha has less beneficial power. However, according to the *Rudrakshajabolopanishad*, the rudrakshas of bigger size are the best and rudraksha of the size of *Badari* Fruit (Jujube) is of middle quality and that of the size of chick-pea is of inferior quality.

In 1864, Lt. Col. Kerber Drvry recorded that the flowering time is in February. However, sadhu lore claims that in Nepal, in an annual cycle, one or two rare one-mukhee rudrakshas are found and the tree often goes without fruit for years. The rudraksha is cleaned, polished and used as beads and rosaries. According to Kerber Drvry "the hard grooved seeds are frequently worn as beads by Brahmins and fakirs and when set in gold are sold as ornaments in England."

Every rudraksha has cells or *mukhees* which differ in number. This is what distinguishes each from the other. After consulting various sources we can conclude that twenty-one varieties exist. Those with five cells are the most abundant and sell very cheaply while the rarest are the 23 and 26 *mukhees.* Imitation rudrakshas are very common and flood the market. Many religious centres like Haridwar and Varanasi have flora similar to the rudraksha which belong to the *Elaeocarpus* family and are called Bhadrakshas.

Dr. Narayandatt Shrimali, an expert in this field, said that the authenticity of a rudraksha can be checked by two tests. One is that if a rudraksha kept between two copper coins or coils, swings, it is genuine. If not, it is a fake. In the second test a true rudraksha is one which will sink in water or milk and a fake one should float. Another school of thought claims that if one places a rudraksha in water it will begin to emanate heat after twenty or twenty-five minutes. However, despite all these tests only experts can identify the true rudraksha.

Rudrakshas are in three colours, red and black are the most common while white is rarely seen. But as Dr. Shrimali states there are yellow rudrakshas as well. Every rudraksha differs from the other by the number of vein-like faces or *mukhees.* Various types of malas or necklaces are made from the rudrakshas of different mukhees which gives them their name. A mala made up of twenty-one mukhee rudraksha is called the *Indra mala.* This is said to be one of the rarest. It is said that only five people own these malas. Moreover, according to the hearsay nothing in this world is unattainable for the person who wears the Indra mala, as it gives him all the wealth he wants as well as fulfils all his desires.

Special mantras accompany the wearing of the rudraksha mala. The *Sivapurana* states the mantras for the purification or *Shuddhikaran* of rudraksha of one to fourteen *mukhees.* The mantra for the one *mukhee* is *om hiring namaha,* two *mukhee, om namaha,* three *mukhee, om kling namaha,* four *mukhee, om hiring namaha,* five *mukhee, om hiring namaha,* six *mukhee, om hiring huang namaha,* seven *mukhee, om huang namaha,* eight *mukhee, om huang namaha,* nine *mukhee, om hirang huang namaha,* ten *mukhee, om hiring namaha,* eleven *mukhee, om hing huang namaha,* twelve *mukhee, om krong shrong roo namaha,* thirteen *mukhee, om hing namaha*, and finally for the fourteen *mukhee*, *om namaha*. However, it is said that even without the chanting of mantras cosmic vibrations envelop the wearer. The *Jabolok Upanishad* further elaborates the mode of wearing the rudraksha. It says that he who wears ten rudraksha on the neck, twenty-two on the head, six in each ear, twelve on each hand, sixteen on each of the upper arms, one on each eye, one on the lock of hair and a hundred and eight on the chest is in reality Sri Nilkantha Paramsiva himself.

The *Bhagavata*, *Sivapurana* and *Smritis* elucidate the individual interpretation of the rudraksha and the significance of each number of *mukhee*. For example it mentions how one can absolve oneself of the sin of a particular crime by wearing a rudraksha of a certain number of *mukhees*. It also explains the ayurvedic, theosophic and materialistic utility of the rudraksha.

The one *mukhee* rudraksha represents Shiva himself and is one of the rarest. This rudraksha represents three symbols of Lord Shiva, the trishula, linga and sarpa or snake. The one who wears this one *mukhee* rudraksha gets remission from Brahmin *hatya* or killing, which is considered the gravest sin. According to the *Tantra Shastras* only the Mahabhogi of Shankar can own this rudraksha. The person who owns the one *mukhee* rudraksha will not lack anything. It enhances the positive thought level and helps to unfold the dimensions of human personality. With this the person is elevated and can become the richest in the land.

The two *mukhee* rudraksha is called *Gaurishankara* which according to the *Shastras* represents *ardha narishwara*, or the image of God and Goddess together. This is generally meant for all Shaivites and it is believed that the one who wears this is absolved from all sins committed intentionally or unintentionally. It controls sexual desire, develops a smooth concentration, mental peace and enhances the growth of philosophic personality which awakens the *Kundalini*. Its hypnotic effect is widely acknowledged.

The three *mukhee* rudraksha represents Agni and Agni represents purification. It is believed that this washes away the sin of *stree hatya* or killing. According to the *Shastras* it cures fever and gives strength to the weak as it makes the wearer active and free from disease. Its powers are such that it can help the unemployed find jobs.

The four-faced or *mukhee* rudraksha symbolises Brahma. It washes away the sin of *nara hatya* or murder of a man. It is believed that this benefits students as it sharpens the mind and increases the ability to absorb and memorise. It also has medicinal qualities and can cure if boiled in milk and given to a mentally retarded person for twenty days.

Kalagni or the fire of death is represented by the five *mukhee* rudraksha. According to a Pauranic source 'one gets remission from sins incurred by eating food which ought not to have been eaten and enjoying a woman who ought not to have been enjoyed.' The *Shastras* say that this is suitable for a person with heart disease and reduces the fear of poisonous snakes. This rudraksha is also prescribed for a person with disturbed mind as it facilitates peace of mind. It is also believed that with this rudraksha a person can win over his enemy.

The six *mukhee* rudraksha stands for Kartikeya, the six-faced god. By wearing this on the right hand one gets rid of all sins including Brahmin *hatya* or murder. The *Tantra Shastra* says that it helps in developing *siddhi* or success in any work. It also shows amazing results in the development of trade. Whoever wears this suffers from no materialistic desires. It cures diseases like hysteria, fainting, blood pressure and feminine problems.

The seven *mukhee* rudraksha represents Kamadeva and has the power to absolve the wearer from sins like the theft of gold. According to the *Jyotish Shastra* it counteracts a child's bad planetary positions. Dr. Shrimali says that whoever wears this rudraksha will not die a violent or premature death. One also gets rid of trauma of *mrigi* or *petimal.*

Vinayaka, the general of the great army, is symbolised by the eight *mukhee* rudraksha. Pauranic sources claim that it has the power to erase deceit such as passing off poor quality rice as genuine, keeping false weights and measures and such forth. The *tantrik* school of thought says that it helps to acquire concentration and mental peace especially if one wants to awaken the *kundalini.* The eight *mukhee* rudraksha suits a businessman especially if he wants to acquire wealth. It also cures paralytic strokes.

The nine *mukhee* rudraksha represents Bhairava and is worn on the left hand. It has the power to make the wearer as mighty as a god which in turn leads to salvation. This is a rare kind as it is the embodiment of the nine powers of the god. It especially suits the devotees of Durga. Pauranic sources claim that it rids a person of the sins incurred by killing a child in the womb a thousand times and killing Brahmins a hundred times. It is also a cure for all diseases related to the heart.

The rare ten *mukhee* rudraksha represents the figure of Janardana and protects the wearer from evil spirits and *brahma rakshs.* It also acts as a protection against snakebite. According to the tantrik interpretations, the ten *mukhee* rudraksha represents Yama and protects the wearer against the ill-effects of tantrik power. It also has great medicinal qualities and can cure a patient of whooping cough if he drinks the milk in which this rudraksha has been stirred thrice.

The eleven *mukhee* rudraksha represents the eleven forms of Shiva. Worn on the head, it bestows upon the wearer the benefits of performing the horse sacrifice. Women generally wear the eleven *mukhee* rudraksha as it not only improves the ability to bear children but also increases the longevity of their husbands. It controls the spread of contagious diseases.

The twelve-faced rudraksha is the dwelling place of the twelve *Adityas.* It is worn on the ear to appease the Sun God. It guards the wearer against any injury incurred from the horns and teeth of animals, various diseases and anxiety. The wearer assumes a god-like aura and is respected by all. According to the *Shastras* the twelve *mukhee* rudraksha also represents Vishnu and is worn by those who aspire to be *brahmacharis* or bachelors. It is believed that the wearer will radiate with brightness and resist the lure of his *indriyas* or senses.

The one who wears the thirteen-faced rudraksha will be equal to Kartikeya. The *Shastras* say that it also represents Kamadeva. Only the very fortunate can wear this rudraksha as it has the ability to fulfil every wish and earns the wearer respect and stability. For those who desire beauty, it should be stirred in milk which is then drunk regularly. The person who wears the fourteen *mukhee* rudraksha is transformed into the real *Paramsiva.* It also represents Tripurari. According to the *Jabolok Upanishad* this is the eye of Shiva. It is a protection against diseases.

The fifteen *mukhee* rudraksha represents Pashupati and benefits those who want spiritual enhancement of mind and body. Its supernatural power guards its owner against theft. The seventeen *mukhee* rudraksha represents the god Vishwakarma. It is believed that the one who wears a mala of this rudraksha will achieve not only sudden wealth but also spiritual power. The earth is symbolised by the eighteen *mukhee* rudraksha. It is specially meant for women and children as it protects the former against premature delivery and the latter against disease.

The nineteen *mukhee* rudraksha embodies Narayana himself. It fulfils all materialistic desires as it sharpens the business acumen. The twenty *mukhee* rudraksha represents Brahma. It enhances knowledge as well as bestows mental peace. It also improves the visual power.

Finally, the twenty-one *mukhee* rudraksha is the rarest of them all, and is the embodiment of Kuber or god of wealth. This is worn by the one who wants to acquire worldly pleasures, happiness and luxury. It makes the wearer rich and negates any kind of adversity.

The *Devi Bhagavatam* says that one is benefited by simply looking at or touching a rudraksha. Many examples prove the splendour or *mahima* of the rudraksha. Swami Sachidanandan said that when the world realises the totality of the rudraksha's *mahima* nothing will be impossible. In England, Paul Hume, in his celebrated study, concluded that nothing is impossible with the rudraksha, it can make one rich, change one's fate as well as hypnotise or influence people. Elsewhere in the world, its therapeutic effect has been positive as it is known to cure diseases like cancer and ease personal trauma.

The rudraksha is thus more than a mere bead or shrub which is found in abundance in the Himalayan region. It has existed through the ages in this ancient land as not only a spiritual symbol but also as a medicinal remedy, a source of materialistic as well as spiritual attainment.

The Sacred Tulsi: Where Vishnu Resides

Ocimum basilicum or *Ocimum sanctum* which is commonly known as Tulsi is one of the holiest and most useful plants of Hindus. It is found everywhere in sandy and uncultivated places. In 1897 J.A. Dubois wrote that "Brahman reveres it as wife of Vishnu and believes that nothing on the earth can equal the virtues of the tulsi." Furthermore, he quoted "*Tulsi-Tulana-Nasty, Ataeva Tulsi*" or the divine Tulsi is incomparable.

There are two types of Tulsi plant—one is *Rama Tulsi* having light green leaves, generally of bigger size and the other *Krishna Tulsi* having dark green leaves which is a prerequisite for the worship of Vishnu and Narayana.

In the famous book "The Pattern of Tree Worship and its Significance" Dr. Sen has quoted P.V. Sharma who traced the origin of tulsi and stated that "there is no mention of Tulsi in Amarakosha. Of course the word *Surasa* is there...it appears that the word *Surasa* was prevalent for Tulsi in ancient period and it was only in the medieval period, probably 9-10th century A.D. that the word Tulsi appeared on the scene but it attained prominence only between 12th and 14th century A.D. It is not improbable that during the natural course of development *Surasa* became Tulsi: *Surasa* > *Surasi* > *Sulasi* > *Chulasi* > *Tulasi*." Thus the word *Surasa* was philologically converted to tulsi.

It is interesting to note that Tulsi, which is worshipped throughout India, is referred with different names. In Sanskrit, Bengali, Gujarati and Marathi it is known as Tulsi. Moreover, in Sanskrit Tulsi is also known as *Maiyarika* and in

Bengali it is also known as *Babultulsi.* Marathi and Oriyan often refer it as *Tulasa* and in Punjabi it is called *Babri.* In Telangana they call it *Bhutulsi,* however sometimes in Andhra it is known as *Tirunapatchi.* Tulsi is also called as *Sabza* in Maharashtra.

The tulsi manifested itself through the course of time and its symbolic culmination encompassed varied names of gods, goddesses, spirits and reincarnations thereof. Hence the Hindus identify Tulsi with varied names like Vishnu, Krishna, Rama, Narayana, Brundavati, Hari, Jagannath, Rai, Damodar, Lakshmi, etc.

The origin of the Tulsi goes back to the *Pauranic* era. Vettam Mani wrote in his *Pauranic Encyclopaedia* that Vishnu had three wives, Saraswati, Lakshmi and Ganga. Saraswati and Lakshmi once had a terrible quarrel and cursed one another. Saraswati's curse transformed Lakshmi into a Tulsi plant, forced to live on earth forever. However, Vishnu intervened and said, "Lakshmi you will live in the world as a holy tulsi and when the curse has been completed you will come back to me. On that day a river Gandaki will start from your body which will be in the shape of the holy Tulsi plant. On the bank of that river, I will remain as a stone image (Salagram Shila)." To commemorate this pauranic legend on the eleventh day of the month of Kartika (Oct.-Nov.) Tulsi is married to Krishna by all Vaishnavites. Moreover, *Tulsi Mahimamritya* noted that Tulsi was born during Purnima of Kartika.

For a Vaishnavite Tulsi is the holiest plant and without its leaves no ceremonial worship of Vishnu is possible. It is praised as destroying all the evils of the present aeon and it is considered sinful to break its branches. Since long Tulsi has remained an integral part of Vaishnavism and the *Bhakta Màla* states that "They who bear the Tulsi round the neck, the rosary of Lotus seeds, have the shell and discus impressed upon their upper arms, and the upright streak along the centre of the forehead, they are Vaishnavas, and sanctify the world." The aim of worshipping Tulsi has varied meanings in different regions. It is gathered that generally widows worship Tulsi for salvation, girls worship it for having good husbands, and couples worship it for getting better children and aged people worship it for finding a place in heaven.

The nineteenth century scholar M. Williams recorded that "In its (Tulsi) roots are contained all places of pilgrimage; its centre contains all the deities and its upper branches all the Vedas." Ritualistically speaking, since time immemorial Tulsi has remained an integral part of Hindu way of life. The puja of Tulsi is offered daily. And the *prasad* of Lord Krishna is a leaf of tulsi. When a Brahmin is dying one of the tulsi plants is fetched and placed on a pedestal. After puja a bit of tulsi is offered to the dying man, and the leaves are placed on his face, eyes, ears and chest; he is then spinkled from head to foot with a tulsi's twig which has been dipped in water. While this ceremony is being performed his friends and relatives chant in high pitch 'tulsi, tulsi'. The man can then die in the happy certainty that he will go to Swarga. *Tulsi Mahimamritya* recorded that if a dying person gets tulsi water he goes to *Vishnu Loka.* It is popularly believed that tulsi even wards off the messengers of *Yama*, the ruler of the dead, who would not enter a house containing a sprig of tulsi. When death occurs the funeral pyre should be constructed of tulsi, palasa and sandalwood.

According to the hearsay if anyone waters the tulsi plant regularly he attains salvation. If one offers a branch of it to Vishnu regularly he achieves salvation after death. If a branch of it is offered to Vishnu in the month of Kartika it will be more pleasing to the God than offering thousand cows. Whosoever offers Tulsi at any time is assured of becoming like Vishnu himself, and of enjoying a share in Vishnu's happiness. Most Brahmins cultivate the plant in their houses and offer it daily prayer. They take care that it should grow near the places they perform their ablution, and in their meeting places such as *Chuttrams.* The tulsi is usually planted on a little mound of sand, which they call *Brindavanam* or on a square pillar of four feet in height, hollow at the top, with its four sides facing the four points of the compass. Brahmins consider it a peculiarly meritorious act to carefully watch and cultivate the plant.

Furthermore, according to *Tulsi Mahimamritya* a touch of Tulsi (*Tulsisparsha*) is comparable to bathing, meditation and takes towards emancipation.

The renowned saint Omkarnath said that if anybody donates Tulsi leaf during the month of Kartika, this *daana* or gift as *prasadam* becomes equivalent to *Godaan* or gift of cow to a Brahmin. Thus we find in all Krishna temples of Vrindabana the *prasad* is Tulsi leaves. Moreover amongst Vaishnavites, it is widely believed that whosoever sports Tulsi wood-mala gets the fruit of *Aswamedh Yagna.* Furthermore, Omkarnath had referred to *Tulsimritika,* or earth beneath the Tulsi plant, as sacred and said that if anybody besmears his body with *Tulsimritika* he gets the merits of best yogi.

The aim and modes of Tulsi worship might differ from region to region but the basic aspiration of emancipation remained the core objective of *Vishnustuti.*

Nairs of Kerala after bath take seven circumbulations of Vrindabana or Tulsithara—a tulsi planted atop the raised masonry. Vaishnavites of Uttar Pradesh, according to B.L. Desai, plant Tulsi on the palm of their hand and with it cover their pilgrimage. However, tulsi worship is not limited to man's theosophical aspirations as Tulsi's curative effect has been widely acknowledged by the Ayurvedic system of medicine, based on the *Atharvaveda.*

Its leaves have a sweet aromatic scent and act as a cough elixir; indeed the Hindus think that they possess many medicinal properties. The Brahmins always swallow one or two leaves after their meals which helps digestion. Tulsi leaves are considered as a potential preventive medicine. As we find the Hindus eat some leaves before and after their ablution in cold water in order to keep up proper temperature in the stomach and prevent ailments arising from cold.

Since long there is a practice among Hindus to put tulsi leaves in cooked food to prevent germination and in stored water to prevent bacteria formation during solar or lunar eclipse. Thus tulsi is widely acknowledged as a great antidote. This theo-medicinal practice has become a part of the cultural ethos and is in vogue all over. Moreover, tulsi plant possesses many curative properties and is an antidote to snake-venom. It is acknowledged a great destroyer of mosquitoes and other pests. Thus every Hindu home cultivates Tulsi in its *angana* or courtyard.

The famous saint Omkarnath once narrated in a discourse that in the 19th century one Englishman, the Chief Electrical Engineer of Calcutta, planted only tulsi plants all around his bungalow. When asked the reason he explained that tulsi plant's electrical strength cannot be compared with any plant of the world and a tulsi plant purifies the air of an area of two hundred metres all around. It destroys Malaria, Plague, Thysis. And if one ties a piece of wood of tulsi plant in any part of the body then the germs of communicable diseases never enter the body. And finally this practice enhances longevity.

Likewise Tulsi has lived down the ages spreading the aroma of its medicinal value and remained as a religio-cultural ethos of Hindu way of life.

The Sacred Bilva Tree

Bilva or Aegle marmelos is the embodiment of Lord Shiva himself and is one of the sacred tree symbols of Hinduism. One finds the reference of this tree throughout India. In Sanskrit this is known as *Bilva* and in Bengali and Hindi this is called *Bel.* In Gujarati Bilva is called *Bili.* In Malayalam this tree is known as *Kuyvalu.* Tamilians call it *Villuvan* and in Telugu Bilva is referred to as *Maredu.*

From the Hindu pantheism point of view this tree is the symbolic representation of Shiva, Parvati, Surya and Lakshmi—the Goddess of Wealth. It is said that no worship of Shiva is complete without offering *Bel patra* or Bilva leaf. Thus Shiva is called *Vilvadanda* or staff of the bel-wood. Indologist Dr. Sankar Sengupta recorded that "These leaves on the lingam cool and refresh the heated deity. Its trifoliate leaf or *tripatra* symbolises the three functions—creation, preservation and destruction—of the Lord as well as His three eyes."

It is forbidden to break the branches of the tree as *Brahmodaitya* or Ghost Gods reside on it. In Bengal during the Durga Puja on the *ashtami* (eighth day) the Goddess Durga is invoked on a twig of Bel tree. And in the prayer a devout says, "I shall get hold of thee and worship thee as the Goddess Durga. Thou art Sriphala. Thou art great virtue, and always dear to Sankara. I welcome thee, in order to invoke the Goddess Chandika." The fruit of Bel tree is also called *Sriphala* because it is said the fruit is made out of the milk of Goddess Sri.

Mahant Rama Shankar of Banaras wrote quoting the *Skanda Purana* and explained the origin of Bilva tree, "One day while Parvati was resting some drops of sweat fell from her forehead on the mountain Mandara, from which grew the bel tree, Girija lives on the root of the tree, Maheswari on its shoulder, Dukshayani on its branches, Parvati among its leaves, Katyayani in its fruit, Gaori in its flowers while in thorns the numerous Saktis find a home. It is also believed that Lakshmi, the Goddess of Wealth, also lives in the bel tree." Those who perform the puja of Shiva and Parvati devoutly, using the leaves, will be endowed with spiritual powers. The leaves are symbols of three *gunas*: *Sattva*, *Rajas* and *Tamas*. The five portions of the tree, the root, bark, leaf, flowers and fruit, also have great medicinal value and are used to cure snakebites.

This Bilva tree is found throughout India and Pakistan and a special variety of this tree is also found in Burma. Mythological sources throw some light on the origin of Bilva tree. It states that "The Gods thought of making storement for yonder Sun who did not shine; they offered a white cow to Surya, thereby they restored his brilliance. The Bilva tree was born at the very reappearance of yonder Sun." Thus bel branches are used in kindling sticks during religious ceremonies symbolically representing light due to its divine origin from the yonder Sun.

From the medicinal point of view Bel fruits are very useful. In the ancient Ayurvedic system of medicine one can find ample references of usefulness of Bel for the cure of habitual constipation, dysentery and dyspepsia. In the *dasamula risht*—the famous Ayurvedic tonic, Bel is one of the ten vital ingredients. According to the Smriti those who wear amulet of Bilva, their offspring is not harmed at the time of birth and misfortune never invades the house.

Really speaking Bilva is medicinally and religiously very powerful. On the one hand it acts as a boost to health and cure for many ailments, on the other hand it has great spiritual significance which permeates the Hindu way of life.

The Sacred Vata Vriksha

The sacred Vata or *Ficus bengalensis* is the most venerated tree among Hindus. Vata or Banyan tree is considered as immortal and is held in great adoration since the Vedic days. Lord Buddha had attained his enlightenment when seated under a Vata Vriksha or Bo-tree. The oldest Vata is found at Prayag where three sacred rivers—Ganga, Jamuna and Saraswati—meet. In ancient scriptures like the *Aitareya Brahmana, Ramayana, Uttar Ramcharit* there is mention about this Vata tree. This sacred tree symbolises Brahma, Vishnu, Shiva, Sasthi, Krishna, Lakshmi, Kuber, Makhadan, etc.

We find the legendary reference of W. Crooke about Vata in the *Brahmapurana* where it is recorded that "Rishi Markandeya had the presumption to ask Narayan to show him a specimen of his delusive power. The God in answer to his prayer drowned the whole world in a sudden flood and only the *Akshya* Vata or imperishable banyan tree raised its head above the water, with a little child seated on its topmost bough, that put out its head and saved the terrified saint just as he was on the point of drowning."

The story about the origin of Vata Vriksha narrates that once Shiva and Parvati were engaged in amorous dalliance in a secluded place where Agni came to crack a joke on the instigation of Brahma, Vishnu and Maheshwara. Parvati became angry and cursed the instigators and immediately Brahma was metamorphosed into Palasa, Vishnu into Peepal and Maheshwara into Vata.

Since time immemorial Vata is being worshipped by the people of the Indian subcontinent and referred to in different names.

In Sanskrit and Bengali this is known as *Vata* or *Akshya Vata.* In Hindi this is called *Bor.* In Gujarati it is known as *Vad.* Marathi devouts call it *Vada.* In Telugu *Vata* is known as *Peddamatti.* In Tamil Nadu it is called *Pudavam.* Finally in Kerala it is known as *Pearl.*

In the month of Jyestha (May-June) women of Maharashtra and Gujarat worship Vad or Vada on the 15th day. In eastern India during *Shasti Puja* Vata branch is a must because this is worshipped on the occasion of 'fertility' puja. Vata is also worshipped as Brahma, thus people of Bengal worship it on every Saturday during Jyestha.

In the famous legendary story of Satyavana-Savitri where on Satyavana's death Savitri fought against Yama—the God of Death, to revive her husband, she is said to have kept Vata-Savitri Vrata or fast on the fifteenth day of Jyestha. It is said Savitri got back the lost life of her husband Satyavana from Yama. Thus womenfolk keep this Vrata for the longevity of their husbands. Moreover, Vata tree is also very popularly known as '*Eccha Vriksha*' or the 'Wish Tree'. Varied forms of medicine are prepared from this tree.

Thus Vata Vriksha stands firm on its ground and remains a strong sign and symptom of Hindu symbology.

The Sacred Peepal Tree

Amongst the sacred trees of India Peepal or *Ficus religiosa* stands foremost. According to common belief Lord Vishnu and other gods reside beneath it. Devout Hindus worship Peepal as they feel this tree is the symbolic representation of various gods and goddesses like Vishnu, Buddha, Krishna, Brahma, Lakshmi, Surya, Aditya, Vana Durga, etc. This tree appears to have been associated with the Mother Goddess in the Indus Valley civilisation. This sacred Peepal finds its mention in the *Rigveda*. According to Vedic sources its wood was used as fire vessels and as drill for producing sacred fire. Peepal is sprinkled with water accompanied by prayers for the removal of certain ills, such as throbbing of the eyes and arms, dreadful dreams, etc.

The Peepal tree is called by nine different names in different languages and geographical settings. In Sanskrit it is called *Bodhi*. In Hindi, Marathi and Punjabi this tree is called *Peepal*. In Bengal this is called *Asvattha* and Gujaratis call it *Piplo*. In Oriyan culture this is *Mui Chitka* tree. In the Deccan, Telugu-speaking devouts call it *Pippali* and in Kanarese this is *Arali*. Finally, the Keralites call it *Al* or *Aryal* in Malayalam language.

The custom of Peepal worship dates back to the Harappan culture and this has also an important position in Brahmanical religion. According to the Hindu scriptures it is said that when *Daityas* or giants had driven out gods and goddesses from the Heaven they took shelter under the Peepal tree. According to the *Padma Purana* Au-Lakshmi, the god of ill-luck, resides in this tree and for this reason the Au-Lakshmi is worshipped by devout Hindus on every Saturday.

This tree is one of the most beautiful trees in the country and grows to a huge size. This is found everywhere, but especially where the Brahmins perform their ablutions. Its large leaves are very soft to touch and are of bright green colour. These leaves are so light and thin that the slightest breeze sets them in motion, and as they produce an impression of most refreshing coolness, the tree is considered to possess health-giving properties.

Various rituals current among womenfolk are connected with the Peepal tree. In Bengal, on the *Sankranti* (the last day of Bengali Calendar) *Asvattha Pata Broto* or fast is observed which is meant to increase happiness and prosperity of the family.

In northern India, on the *Somavati Amavasya* worshippers pour water and unboiled milk on the roots and make circumbulation of the tree 108 times. In Rajputana, married women worship the Peepal to avoid widowhood. Peepal is also symbolic of ancestors' worship during October-November when earthen pitcher is hung to its branches and filled with water, milk, *Til* and honey. It is believed that ancestors come down from the tree and accept the offerings.

The Peepal tree is also significant from the medicinal point of view. According to the *Ayurveda*, decoction of its bark with honey is good for cure of skin diseases. It is said that "Asvattha bark is useful in gonorrhoea, ulcer and various other skin diseases." From the dried fruit of this tree a powder is prepared and dissolved in water and taken twice a week to cure the deadly disease asthma.

Ritualistically speaking, Hindu women worship Peepal for the boon of male offspring. According to the *Atharva Veda* Peepal tree is considered as benefactor of mankind by blessing barren women with children. Thus the tree is considered potent with fertility. So we can see that Peepal tree is worshipped for its multifarious medicinal and utilitarian value as well.

The Sacred Kadali Tree

Kadali or Kela which is botanically known as *Musa sapientum* (*Musa paradisca*) symbolically represents Lakshmi, Sakambhari, Vana Durga, etc. Banana leaves symbolise coolness and composure. On a higher philosophical plane this tree represents a combination of "*Tatva Jnana*" or eternal knowledge. It may be interesting to note that the trunk of the banana plant is made of multiple layers. If one starts peeling the layers one would reach a point wherefrom nothing would be left to remove. Thus this symbolically suggests that the quest and process of our inner urge for real knowledge goes on by pronouncing '*neti-neti*'—not this, not this!

Ritualistically speaking this Kadali tree is very popular among Hindus especially in Bengal. This tree also has many names. In Sanskrit and Tamil this is called Kadali and in Hindi and Bengali it is known as Kela and Kola respectively.

During September-October on the full-moon day this tree is worshipped along with Lakshmi Puja. Kela tree is also an essential part of Durga Puja. Kadali is said to be the wife of Brahma also. During Durga Puja different plants are collected, for example, Turmeric, Barley, Wood Apple, the Pomegranate, the Asoka, the Paddy and one Kadali plant is bathed and tied together with a creeper plant called *aparajita*, and robed in red *Sari* known as *Kalabau*. This configuration of *Naba-patrika* is the wife of Lord Ganesha. This forms part of the vegetation deities of prehistoric Bengal.

During Puja ceremonies *Naibedya* or offering to the God is done on the *Kadali* leaf. In southern India, the practice of serving food on this leaf is still in vogue which not only provides sumptuous taste but also hot food served on the leaf is said to be having a medicinal effect as chemical effect takes place with chlorophyll.

The whole banana tree is very useful and no part of it is considered useless. Its fruit, both unripe and ripe, flower, its stem are pure healthy food. According to Chintaharan Chakraborty, a renowned scholar, "In Madras, when premature delivery takes place, the child is laid on a plantain leaf smeared with oil, the leaf is changed daily, and the baby is thus treated for the period which is less than the normal time of delivery." These leaves are very useful also for healing of wound and ulcer.

Thus Banana tree has lived down the ages as a symbol of mythological Goddess and the vegetation pantheon which has enormous food and medicinal value as well.

Mango Tree

Mango or *Aam* tree is one of the sacred tree symbols of Hinduism. Five leaves of this tree in a pot which are besmeared with *sindoor* or vermilion is a common site in any Hindu religious ceremony. Throughout India this tree is planted and worshipped by devouts. With the passage of time this tree acquired many names. In Sanskrit mango tree is called *Amra* and in Hindi and Bengali this is called *Aam.* In Gujarat this tree is called *Amlo* and Tamilians call it *Mamaran.* Telugu-speaking people describe it as *Amramu.* In Kerala this is called *Mram* or *Mavu.*

Since the days of the Puranas the *aam* tree is personified with various Gods, Goddesses and spirits. According to the research scholars, in *Aam* Vriksha, Lakshmi, Govardhan, Gandharva and fertility God reside.

Aam leaf smeared with *sindoor* (vermilion) is called *amer pallav* and is kept in a pot called *Lakshmi Ghata.* This *Ghata* or pot personifies Lakshmi herself. Branches of mango tree are also used in Yagna or sacrifice. In every puja at house the mango branches, leaves and *Lakshmi Ghata* are a must and counted as auspicious. Moreover, mango leaves are widely used in marriage ceremonies as these leaves are termed as *Kama* or fertility God. In some parts of India these leaves are tied on a swinging thread hung on the front door ritualistically signifying that some auspicious ceremony is going on in the house.

Aam has medicinal value and its fruit, ripe or unripe, cures many diseases. Thus ritualistically and medicinally mango tree is a household name for every devout Hindu.

Betel Leaf or Pan

Pan plays a very prominent role in socio-religious life of Hindus. There can be no auspicious occasion without *pan.* From a marriage song of eastern India it is gathered that the birth-place of *pan* is the Himalayas. It is said that Shiva and Parvati had sown the seeds of *Pan.* In April-May this sacred betel leaf is worshipped by the *Barui,* a group of pan cultivators of Bengal.

In a marriage ceremony a ritual called *Briddhi-Sraddha* is performed where the bridegroom accepts the bride in name of departed souls of their ancestors. At this point, in the ancestral worship, thirty-two *pan* or betel leaves are required.

According to S. Sengupta, an authority on sacred trees, "Betel leaf is considered sacramental in Hindu religion. Its different positions stand for different symbols and it is said to be the seat of Goddess Lakshmi, i.e., Goddess of Wealth. It is said in *Rajnirghantha* that the very tip of the leaf stands for longevity, and basal portion is for fame, and the middle portion is the seat of Goddess Lakshmi. So chewing the middle portion (of *pan*) is a taboo to the Hindus." Furthermore, ancient scriptures opine that *pan* or betel leaf increases passion, sweetens the breath, and cures diseases of mouth.

According to Ayurvedic science, the betel leaf is very useful in cure of diseases which are caused by air, bile and phlegm. *Vaidyas* or physicians state that its juice is very helpful in curing various diseases. It is said that if it is fixed on the forehead it cures headache. The heated pan-juice, if poured in the infected ear, prevents pus formation. *Pan* is good for cure of cough, cold, etc. Thus *Pan* has become a part of Hindu life and remains a symbol of spiritual veneration as well.

Apart from these sacred trees and plants there are many more sacred trees worth mentioning. Some of them are Durba Grass, Soma, Karpura, etc. Let us course through them briefly.

Durba Grass

Durba Grass stands foremost in *Puja* ceremony, and in *Yagna* this grass is used for each offering to Gods. The Pujari or the priest must invoke this grass and makes a ring which he wears round his finger throughout the course of the religious rites.

Botanically this Durba grass is referred to as *Poa cynosuroides* and belongs to the genus borge. It is found everywhere, especially in dams or marshy fields. It grows up to two-foot height and has three sharp blades at the top. Every devout Hindu cultivates this grass in his courtyard.

However, scholars differ about the origin of Durba grass. One school of thought states that this sacred Durba grass was produced at the time when the Gods and Asuras (evil spirits) were busy churning with the mountain Mandara the sea of milk in order to extract nectar or *Amrita*, which would render them all immortal. Another school of thought opines that when Gods were drinking *Amrita* or nectar desperately a few drops of *Amrita* had fallen on this grass which made this Durba grass a sacred one. Thus goes the story of Durba which from time immemorial remained sacred and found its pronounced prominence in all the ritualistic ceremonies of the Hindus.

Soma Plant

Soma plant or *Sarcostemns acdium* is also very prominent among the Hindu sacred symbols. Soma plant is the personification of Moon. Soma tree provides a divine, milky narcotic juice. This tree is divine in nature and spiritual in value which used to be offered in oblation to God.

The recipe or the process of preparation of Soma *rasa* has been elaborated by Dr. Sengupta, "For the preparation of liquor the creeper be crushed in a mortar with pestle, water is added to it. It is pressed and the juice is extracted with fingers. Then it is allowed to pass through a sieve made of sheep wool. After filtering, it is offered to Gods." Since the Vedic ages drinking has never been dubbed as a vice. And even in the later period of history we find the consumption of soma rasa was common. Literary works of Kalidas give ample references of even women enjoying the drinks.

Sacred Karpura

Karpura or camphor is another important sacred plant which has more than 60 synonymous names and is of immense spiritual and medicinal value. Karpura is also a symbol of Moon. Shine and coolness is more respected feature of Karpura. Thus camphor is a must for performing marriage rites. Especially, this is used in *Havana* or *Yagna*. The *Susruta-Samhita* has mentioned in detail about Karpura. This is useful for removal of bad odour from the mouth. In the Sutras the juice of the tree was considered as forbidden drink—but Karpura and Soma were allowed to be consumed as drink. This is also worshipped as any other Hindu deity.

Sacred Flowers

We have seen there are numerous sacred trees which are subject of human adoration and symbolise Gods, Goddesses and spirits.

However, no Hindu worship of Gods and Goddesses can be thought of without offering them flowers. It is interesting to note that particular flowers are associated with particular deities and the colour of the flower matters most.

Likewise, when a devout worships Shiva China Roses are essential. Vishṇu is worshipped with white flowers. Mango-blooms symbolically represent *Kama Deva.* In *Shakti* cult red flowers like *jaba* are mandatory for the worship of Kali and Chamundi. During Kali Puja in Bengal, the idol is garlanded with a mala or necklace of 108 *jaba* flowers. The lotus is used for Sun God, Saraswati and Durga. The sanctity of lotus may be traced to the mythological story that Brahma, the Creator of this Universe, was born on the lotus issuing from the navel of Vishnu. Planet Saturn is worshipped with blue flowers.

Thus every God is worshipped with sacred flowers and trees which are part of Hindu rites. Thematically they are a mixture of spiritual and worldly aspirations of a devout Hindu.

Select Bibliography

Primary Sources

Bhasmajabalopanisad (Saiva Upanisad), Madras, 1950.
Brahma Sutra, Bombay, 1934.
Brhajjabalopanisad (Saiva Upanisad), Madras, 1950.
Devi Bhagavata Purana, Calcutta, 1958.
Isopanisad, The Principal Upanisads by S. Radhakrishnan, London, 1953.
Kathopanisad, The Principal Upanisads by S. Radhakrishnan, London, 1953.
Krsnopanisad (Vaisnava Upanisads), Madras, 1953.
Linga Purana, Manuska Roy, Calcutta, 1960.
Manu Smriti, Benaras, 1953.
Mundakopanisad, The Principal Upanisads by S. Radhakrishnan, London, 1953.
Nyaya Sutras, Poona, 1939.
Padma Purana, Calcutta, 1958.
Rgveda Ed. S.P.D. Satvalekar, Bombay, 1954.
Rudraksajabalopanisad (Saiva Upanisads), Madras, 1950.
Siva Upanisad, The Unpublished Upanisads, Madras, 1933.
Visnu Purana, Samvata, Poona, 1890.

Encyclopaedias and Dictionaries

Encyclopaedia Americana, Vol. VI, New York.
Encyclopaedia Britannica, Vol. 8, London, 1955.
Encyclopaedia of Religion and Ethics, New York, 1955.
Encyclopaedia, Pauranic by Vettam Mani, Benaras, 1964.
(An) Encyclopaedia of Religion by M.A. Canny, Delhi, 1976.
Encyclopaedia of Superstition and Folklore (Reprint), Detroit, 1971.
Amarakosa(m), Benaras, 1957.
A Sanskrit-English Dictionary (Reprint), Delhi, 1972.

A Dictionary of Symbols by (Tr.) Cirlot, J.E., London, 1962.

A Classical Dictionary of Hindu Mythology and Religion, Geography, History and Literature (Reprint), New Delhi, 1967.

A Glossary of Colloquial Anglo-Indian Words and Phrases, and of Kindred Terms, Etymological, Historical, Geographical and Discursive (First Published 1886: Hobson-Jobson).

Secondary Sources

Bhattacharyya, A., "Popular Nature Worship in Bengal", *Indian Folklore*, April-June, 1959.

Bhowmick, P.K., *Occultism in Trienge Bengal*, Calcutta, 1978.

Birdwood, G.C.M. (Sir), *The Arts of India* (Reprint), N. Delhi, 1988.

Chakraborty, Chintaharan, *Hindur Achar Anusthan*, Calcutta (1377 Bengali Era).

Chakravorty, T.K. & Sarkar, P., "Medicinal Plants", *Science Reporter*, India, June, 1980.

David T. (Tr.), *Hieun Tsang Wrote (629-645 A.D.)*, London, 1961.

Dubois, J.A. Abbe, *Hindu Manners, Customs & Ceremonies*, Oxford, 1897.

Fergusson, James, *Rude Stone Monuments in All Countries: Their Ages and Uses*, London, 1872.

In the Image of Man, "Tree, Flowers, Foliage", Great Britain, 1982.

Jit, Inder "Indu", *Science of Symbols: Deeper View of Indian Deities*, New Delhi, 1978.

Kane, P.V., *History of Dharma Sastra*, Poona, 1962.

Mahajan, V.D., *Ancient India*, New Delhi, 1965.

Mahant Rama Shankar, "Symbols of Shiva", *The India Magazine*, June, 1988.

Marshall, J., *Mohenjo-daro and the Indus Valley Civilization*, London, 1931.

Matt, Leonard Von, *The Art of the Etruscans*, London, 1969.

Mckenzie, Jone, *Hindu Ethics*, Oxford University Press, 1922.

Morgan, W.K., *Religion of the Hindus*, Ronald, 1953.

Omkarnath Thakur, *Tulsimahimamritya*, Calcutta.

Presler, H. Henry, *Primitive Religion in India*, The Senate of Serampore College & The Christian Literary Society, 1971.

Priestley, H.E., *Britain under the Romans*, London, 1967.

Radhakrishnan, S., *Eastern Religion and Western Thought*, Oxford, 1939.

Radhakrishnan, S., *Indian Philosophy*, London, 1958.

Rawal, A.J., *Indian Society, Religion & Mythology*, N. Delhi, 1982.

Sastri, K.N., *The New Light on the Indus Valley Civilization*, Vol. II, Delhi.

Sengupta, S., *Sacred Trees Across Cultures & Nations*, Calcutta, 1980.

Sharma (Dr.), T.R., *Studies in the Sectarian Upanishad*, Benaras, 1972.

Shrimali, Narayan Datt, 'Rudraksha', *Dharmayug*, 1979 June (*sic*).

Vivekananda, Swami, *Complete Works of Swami Vivekananda,* Vols. 1-8, Advaita Ashram, 1960.

Westall, William, *The Hindoos,* London, 1847.

Williams, Monier, *Buddhism in its connection with/its contrast with Christianity,* London, 1889.

(The) World's Great Religion, Life, New York, 1957.

Index